Praise for *Others Will Enter the Gates*

"*Others Will Enter the Gates* is a timely and necessary collection and to say that it is thought-provoking and versatile is an understatement. I urge everyone who cares about and loves the exiled and immigrant voices that constantly provide the new blood that keeps contemporary American Poetry lively and exciting to read and share this book, and to the teachers I say please don't miss out on this great opportunity to use this wonderful collection in your courses."
—Virgil Suárez

"Each time I open this book, each time I follow one of these fine poets through another gate in this country of a thousand gates, I feel like an immigrant again, realigned with my own Huguenot ancestors fleeing the religious tyrannies of France three centuries ago. To read these essays is to have your faith in the poetic future of this land restored, over and over again."
—David Shumate

" *Others Will Enter the Gates* is a multilayered exploration by writers of different generations and backgrounds that passionately offers an urgent and daring insight into America's ever-expanding literature on the immigrant experience."
—Dike Okoro

"The great irony and most fabulous beauty of this very real and readable collection of essays are testament to why poetry has lasted for tens of thousands of years. No matter one's circumstance, it's outlived everything—every economic theory, every political ideology. Poetry exists because it is the language for which we have no language. What do we do when we can't explain profound and genuine grief? What do we do when we can't articulate profound and genuine joy? These poets, like all poets, make poems."
—Ralph Angel

Others Will Enter the Gates

Immigrant Poets on Poetry, Influences,
and Writing in America

Edited by Abayomi Animashaun

Introduction by Kazim Ali

Black
Lawrence
Press

Black
Lawrence
Press

www.blacklawrence.com

Executive Editor: Diane Goettel
Book design: Amy Freels
Cover art: "Buddhapur Ana VI" © 2014 by Catherine Eaton Skinner

Published 2015 by Black Lawrence Press.
Printed in the United States.

Let America be America Again © 2013 by Danielle Legros Georges. First appearing in *Mass Poetry*. Reprinted by permission of the author.

In The Name Of The Letter, The Spirit & The Double Helix © 2014 by Fady Joudah. First appearing in *The Kenyon Review*. Reprinted by permission of the author.

Selections from *The Pillow Book* © 2014 by Jee Leong Koh. First appearing in *PN Review* in 2011, *The Pillow Book* was published in book form by Math Paper Press in 2012, and in an illustrated English-Japanese bilingual edition by Awai Books in 2014. Selections appeared in *Manoa: A Pacific Journal of International Writing* in 2014. Reprinted by permission of the author.

The Reader Within Me © 1999 by Majid Naficy. First appearing in *Muddy Shoes* by Majid Naficy, Beyond Baroque Books. Reprinted by permission of the author.

Christopher Columbus Was A Damn Blasted Liar © 2014 by Matthew Shenoda. First published in *Guernica*. Reprinted by permission of the author.

Contents

II: Language

III: Influences

Preface

No anthology on writing, conceived for the purpose of print, whether of prose or poetry, can be exhaustive. This is because not *all* writers can be featured due, among other concerns, to the realities of scope and space *and* of merit and purse. Instead, the idea behind this project was to be panoramic, to bring as many immigrant poets into an anthology, whose main aim is to answer the question: How do émigré poets in the United States make sense of their immigrant experiences? To frame the discourse, the following areas of focus were suggested in the original call for submissions: a) *Influences* b) *What it means to be a poet in America* c) *How work fits within the American poetic tradition* and d) *How work fits within the poetic tradition of the (poet's) home country.*

The immigrant experience, however, is not neat and tidy. Thus, instead of squarely fitting in, most of the pieces in this anthology challenge and blur those categories in the call for submissions. In some cases, poets simply used one of the four categories as launching pads into more pressing concerns; in others, poets addressed two or more categories; and so on. Whatever fancies one held about straightforward categorizations were quickly dispelled. Also, each contributor's unique perspective on the experience of the émigré poet in America is a reminder, however commonplace the idea, that when it comes to immigrant poets in America, or immigrants for that matter, there is no monolith.

Still, to allow for ease of navigation, the pieces in this anthology have been separated into five categories: *Self-Definition, Language, Influences, The Émigré Poet in America,* and *A Third Space.* These categories feel more suited to the pieces submitted for the collection. They feel less imposed. But, they are by no means absolute; because, which émigré poet in America has not wrestled with self-definition? Which has not, in some form, grappled with the dilemma of language or explored how influences from the home and new countries (terms here used loosely) speak to each other and affect her/him? Not to mention that the metaphor of *the third space* is one that many immigrants, poets and non-poets alike, find useful in conceptualizing their variegated experiences.

Also, readers will notice, and quickly too, that many of the pieces could easily have been placed in other, equally viable, categories. Just as the categories are not absolute, the arrangement and placement of the essays are not either. That said, it is no secret that the title of this collection of essays, *Others Will Enter the Gates,* is taken from the second section of Walt Whitman's "Crossing Brooklyn Ferry", a stanza that carries a ring of the prophetic. However, despite the poem's auguries, one cannot ignore present day realities—the fact that even as this preface is being written undocumented immigrants are being detained, that others are denied entry into the United States, and that many *do not* enter the gates.

An immense gratitude to all who have supported this project at the beginning and at various points, especially Folabo Ajayi, Fred Marchant, Kim Stafford, and Naomi Shihab Nye. Also, thanks to the contributors for their engaging pieces. Thanks to Kazim Ali for his patience and his introduction. Thanks too to the hardworking people at Black Lawrence Press and to Diane Goettel for believing in this project from the outset. Above all, thanks to Angela Leroux-Lindsey, a person of intelligence, vision, and kindness; wit, principle, and rigor, who was as much an equal partner as she was a co-editor in the long journey of bringing this collection to fruition. Without her, this anthology would not be possible.

Abayomi Animashaun
Green Bay, WI
January 2015

*Changing
borders*

Introduction

When a body crosses its first border—from inside another body and out into the world—it is *documented,* by a name, a gender, given a nationality (usually), its paternity notated. When we attain consciousness, how much is defined and shaped by this documentation? And who are we beyond that, intrinsically, in our flesh and breath and bones? Anything? The answer to the question matters because what then happens when we *change*—when we cross other borders, into other countries, languages, names and origins?

To move across a national border into another cultural context, to eat food from a different place, to put clothes on or take them off—these things *matter* because the body is an experiential location not a fixed phenomenon. Age and death teach us that much, and quickly, if their other lessons are harder to absorb. *Others Will Enter the Gates* collects a range of voices of immigrant poets to muse on these and other questions. In its prologue Danielle Legros Georges makes an argument against a monocultural or linear understanding of immigration—it is not a singular transition but a moment in process throughout one's life. She contextualizes this in American poetry by looking at such quintessentially "American" poets as Phillis Wheatley and Emma Lazarus, two earlier "immigrant" poets, though the circumstances by which they came to American shores was radically different. She writes that American poetry "defies the monoculture America never truly was."

Many of the poets whose essays are collected in this powerful anthology testify to the fact that crossing borders can be a "lethal" proposition—one can, as when crossing the mythological river Lethe, forget one's language, even one's self. In the opening section, the poets try to frame or problematize the notion of identity to begin with. How is it constructed by language? What limitations or possibilities are inherent in these arrangements? These are some of the questions tackled by the essays in Section 1, "Self-Definition."

Poets often confront and engage this hybridity and multiplicity in various ways. Megan Fernandes, as an African Goan, gravitated toward those poets who worked against neat categorization, poets such as Jorie Graham, Medbh McGuckian and Eleni Sikelianos. She ties her interest in these poets and forms not only to her own cultural background but to a deeper historical context: "I was curious about the hybridity of languages, the way in which Portugal, as one of Europe's oldest borders, allowed for a complex political and literary identity to make its way into imagery, tone and poetic forms." This complexity of identity manifests not only in the content of a poet's work but often in her approach to form. Sun Yung Shin, who came to the United States as an adoptee, writes in an innovative piece of her legal status as a family of one; with no forebear to mark her she has complete freedom for self-invention. She has the papers to prove it.

Zubair Ahmed, interestingly, claims that he found himself as a poet "when [he] stopped thinking in Bengali and switched to thinking in English." The new language, with its unfamiliarity and unmoored from detritus of the past, appeared to help the poet find ways to say things *newly*. It's precisely his in-between state that annealed poetic diction and expression into his mouth of new language.

In contrast, Anis Shivani critiques too easy a reliance on that trope. "One is always a citizen of one or another world," he contends. And in fact goes on to suggest, "Why let go of a convenient pain, which is actually a position of privilege? ... The immigrant poet is allowed to skate history, or rather, choose to withhold it if necessary, because her pain of emigration is supposed to make us cut her some slack." Shivani goes on to interrogate and critique the notion of an "immigrant identity" and to also critique the "benefits" of embracing such an identity.

Maria Victoria Grageda-Smith agrees, at least insofar as it comes to the notion of who is included or excluded from consideration in current discourse on poetry. Regarding Richard Blanco, who recited poetry at Barack Obama's second inauguration, she writes, "There is nothing distinctly Latino or 'immigrant' in Blanco's poem apart from the persona of the poet himself." Smith goes on to consider what the nature of the canon is in American poetry and how poets working in hybrid contexts of culture or language may or may not fit into it.

Rigoberto González, on the other hand, born in Bakersfield, California, resists definition as either an "American" writer or as a "Mexican-American" writer. Instead he chooses to identify as Chicano, "a term that situates [him] politically and geographically within the borders of the United States." Gonzalez points out that to identify as an American would "erase" important forces that have shaped him as a "citizen and artist." He goes on to interrogate the vexed relationship that he has to questions of translation and code-switching, two notions quite embraced by other writers in this anthology.

Kwame Dawes talks about his own multiple backgrounds in Ghana, Jamaica and his current embracing of the identity "African-American" which he had resisted for many years. He does say, "it was a political decision, not an emotional one." Dawes continues to investigate what implication this pluracination has upon his life, in both practical and philosophical valences, as a writer.

Dawes is unsatisfied, in the end, with the limits his *documents*— birth certificate, passport, citizenship papers—place on his true identity: he is unable to be considered as a Jamaican writer, which is the one identity that resonates most truly to him. For every definition, there is a pigeonholing that occurs, preventing the writer—*any* writer—from openness in expression and reception of that expression. Perhaps Shivani is right? And in considering Gonzalez' immigrant experience one remembers that old slogan "I didn't cross the border, the border crossed me."

Of course, immigrant poets may face a kind of pigeon-holing by readers and critics in both their use of language and chosen content, as Michael Dumanis points out in his essay, and his point makes me wonder how indeed "Michael Dumanis" might have been read or critically encountered had he chosen to publish under his original name: Mikhail Edouardovich Dumanis. He acknowledges though that while his own writing and approach to language is situated in an American literary context it does indeed draw from the Russian poetry he found on his parents bookshelves, "wildly declarative and loud in its rhythms, attentive to its surfaces, dramatic in its content, ambitious in its tackling of heady subjects … breathlessly full-throttle, full of sonic energy and internal rhyme."

In the anthology's second section, "Language," poets worry more about the specific implication of the "translation" process on the body and language of the poet. Fady Joudah wonders in his lyrical essay about what is born in such transference, or borne across into the new language. To him, time, money and politics play as much a relationship in the creation and recreation process of the individual human body as the actual distance in miles, the differences in food, clothing and weather. Later on in this book, Pauline Kaldas talks about that process like this: "I circle the immigrant experience—no longer a journey from one location to another but one that wraps around itself overlapping lives and histories."

The body of the immigrant poet thus becomes a transformative and *translating* agent of language and culture, those constructions of identity. Andrei Guruianu picks up Shivani's resistances to the strictures this role may place on the aesthetic development of a poet when he declares, "I sometimes feel as if I'm playing my own character, the embodiment of an 'I' whom everyone watches from a distance but who is nothing more than a flimsy façade."

Of course Guruianu and Shivani are right in a way: there is nothing essentialist about the position of the immigrant other than his arrival. Even in one's own country one can be alienated in both language and culture from the mainstream dominant group. And in this book too, we talk about "gates"—whether one is the keeper of them or the one who enters through with proper permission and documents or whether one is a gatecrasher, as it were. So the key concept is the "crossing" of that gate, the *translation* of one's own self.

The process is not just an alchemy in the poem, it is transformative for the poet. Cristián Flores García discusses this in her essay. Rather than the new language changing her poetry, she claims that "Poetry gave me English." It's *in* poetry that she finds a new home. As Darwish once wrote, decrying the exile of the Palestinian people,

"My homeland is not a suitcase." Later, after more than two decades of living in various cities around the world, he revised his line wistfully, "My homeland is a suitcase."

Piotr Gwiazda shares his own concern with the idea of translation. He quotes Celan as saying, "In a foreign tongue the poet lies." Yet both Celan and Gwiazda write in foreign tongues. Gwiazda goes on to cite Yoko Tawada, a Japanese-born writer who writes in German and relies on what she calls "exophony," "a merging of two linguistic strata that can produce unique variations of syntax, diction, rhythm, accent, and so on." These possibilities in the new language brought from the old seems to be one of the greatest gifts of the transitional position.

Vasyl Makhno points out the large numbers of writers who come to America to live but still write and publish in their own native languages and countries and that their literary lives unfold against those far contexts: "The next time I'm asked what it means to be a Ukrainian poet in America, I want to answer right away with a question: and what does it mean to be a Ukrainian poet in Ukraine?"

In the third section, "Influences," several poets consider their sometimes difficult and oppositional relationships to the canons of their old nations and their new one. Gerardo Pacheco Matus wonders what happens to the poet who draws fully from the Anglo-American tradition when a more hybrid context is what is expected from teachers, critics, readers? Matus feels sometimes criticized for fully embracing the Western canon and must himself reconceptualize his relationship to new Latino writing.

Like Zubair Ahmed, some poets view the complicated political context of exile-in-language to be a position of power. Jose Rodriguez recounts a moment working with school children when he realized that his greatest influence in poetry was a name he didn't even think to share when talking about poetry. Two other poets, Abayo Animashaun and Ilya Kaminsky explore fully the influences of their poetic forebears, from their original home and their new one.

It might be easy to think of the immigrant as *displaced* or *unhomed,* but of course we know that one of the very real things that happens is either assimilation or acclimatization to the new country. In the opening essay of section four, "The Émigré Poet in America," Matthew Shenoda muses on the ways the literature of the new country affects or changes what has been left behind. For Shabnam Piryaei, an exile from Iran, at the beginning poetry itself accompanied her. So embedded in daily life in Iran, the poetry she was so devoted to only heightened her sense of loneliness in America, where it occupies such a peripheral place. Marilène Phipps-Kettlewell can offer Piryaei only cold comfort: "To be a poet is to charm. To be a poet is to console. To be a poet is to silence."

Barbara Jane Reyes has a different view of the artifact of experience, the documents that Sun Yung Shin uses to place herself: "My history, and my family history have always had documents and artifacts: posed and candid photographs, home movies, report cards, detention slips we forged with my parents' signatures, diplomas and degrees, marriage certificates, evidence of immunization, naturalization papers, Philippine and American passports, Facebook posts, and Instagram accounts." She goes on to discuss how the poetry of mythology and oral tradition works against the solidification of identity that these documents—hard copy and electronic—otherwise engender.

In a break from the somewhat more theoretical conversations in the other essays, Ocean Vuong recounts his move to New York City as a young man with $564 in his pocket and little else. Like many of the other essayists he breaks off his narrative digressions several times by saying "We'll save that for another essay." It is as if the plurality of each experience is always already too much for a single try.

In the closing section, "A Third Space," the essays try to formulate what new possibilities their border-crossing has wrought. Lisa Birman came from an English-speaking country and so she does not share the same language conflict shared by many of the other poets, though perhaps because of this she still feels—and admits she will perhaps *always* feel—in an in-between state: "I never meant to leave Australia on a permanent basis. I am still unconvinced that I have."

On the other hand, Sholeh Wolpé, like Anis Shivani, is wary of looking backward: "Shadows have a way of following their makers and questions can be more dangerous than facts." Still, Wolpé—who like many others in the anthology, is actually *unable* to return "home"—confesses in heartbreaking and contradictory parentheticals, "This is (not) my country … They call me an immigrant writer when I am a native of this land." America *has* to be her home because she has no other.

Poetry may then come from that place of defamiliarization—of language and culture—and as such as strangely more easily accessible to those who have crossed such borders into strange lands. Ewa Crusciel extends Ahmed's notion when she suggests that "we can have a new beginning in a new language." Her essay goes on to explore the third language—the one that the poet herself creates in between the mother tongue and the new language.

Of course, sometimes the linguistic differences are not so much political as very, very personal: Vandana Khanna talks of the language barrier between she and her grandmother: "My grandmother spoke no English and my Hindi often stumbled from my lips, clumsy and uncertain …" It's Khanna who understands then, "I can belong to more than one place … I don't have to choose."

Jee Leong Koh considers this problem of belonging in his lyrical essay while Majid Naficy explains, "My body lived in LA but my soul was still rummaging through the ruins of a lost revolution in Iran." In his poems he finds the Pacific and the Caspian merging in ways that confuse and disturb him. And not only has his subjects blurred, but the *reader* he brought with him from Iran has also changed: "He does not want to live in the past."

Pauline Kaldas is, like me, part of what she called the "one-and-a-half immigrant generation," children who arrive with their parents, having spent the earlier part of their lives elsewhere and arriving in the new country in older childhood. She writes at a different angle than Reyes, also part of this generation, on the so-called American Dream—that for many in this generation, the pressures are extreme—familial expectations to adhere to the older traditions vie with growth and identity with the new culture.

Since several of the previous essays have examined how the "immigrant" writer is *received* by the larger readership, it is interesting that David McLoghlin doesn't even identify with being an "immigrant" because, as he points out, "In Ireland, the verb has been outward-bound for hundreds of years." He challenges Pacheco Matus by admitting, "I want it both ways: I want to be free of the constraining aspects of my tradition, but free also to use (or abuse) it in ways that suit me."

In the end I can only come back to my own body, born in England to immigrant parents there, taken back to India and then on to Canada when Trudeau opened the borders, and then following jobs to the United States. As an adult my restless body continues its wandering, not as a tourist, but to live and work—all over the United States from the Hudson Valley to Washington, DC, to San Francisco and the Southwest as well as across the world—to France, Spain,

Palestine, India, Uruguay, Israel—it is in that wandering that I find myself, in that loneliness of perception does my writing then reveal.

Nerval once said that you ought to travel so much that even your home becomes strange to you, but I have no hope other than the opposite—that is to say: once you cross borders often enough you find really that *every* place must be somehow home. The poets collected here testify, both in these statements and in their own work, that such a home is possible.

Kazim Ali
Oberlin, OH
December 2014

Others will enter the gates of the ferry, and cross from shore to shore,
Others will watch the run of the flood-tide,
Others will see the shipping of Manhattan north and west, and the
heights of Brooklyn to the south and east,
Others will see the islands large and small,
Fifty years hence, others will see them as they cross…
—Walt Whitman, "Crossing Brooklyn Ferry"

Others Will Enter the Gates

Immigrant Poets on Poetry, Influences,
and Writing in America

Prologue

Let America be America Again

Danielle Legros Georges

> *O, let America be America again—*
> *The land that never has been yet—*
> —Langston Hughes

American writers (by that I mean U.S. writers) have long pursued the identity and idea of America (by America I mean the United States). The Frenchman-turned-American, Jean de Crèvecoeur, writing in New York shortly before the American Revolution, asks "What is an American?" in his *Letters from an American farmer*. Published in 1782, his book is written from the perspective of a fictional character corresponding to an English friend, in letters, or essays, ranging in subject matter from slavery to an emerging American identity. De Crèvecoeur writes:

> What then . . . is this new man? He is either an [*sic*] European, or the descendant of an European, hence that strange mixture of blood, which you will find in no other country. I could point out to you a family whose grandfather was an Englishman, whose wife was Dutch, whose son married a French woman, and whose present four sons have now four wives of different nations. *He* is an American . . .

Phillis Wheatley, a Gambian- or Senegalese-turned-American woman, published her first and only volume, *Poems on Various Subjects, Religious and Moral*, in 1773. In it appears the poem "On being brought from Africa to America," one of her rare comments on slavery. While Wheatley's Americanness was not chosen by her (she had been kidnapped as a child), her dark Americanness (or perhaps *Un-Americanness*) was central to the nation's economic development. She writes as an American non-citizen (prior to 1776 because the U.S. had yet to be born; and after its birth by virtue of her race and gender). She writes also out of the precarious state of enslavement in Boston:

> Twas mercy brought me from my Pagan land,
> Taught my benighted soul to understand
> That there's a God, that there's a Saviour too:
> Once I redemption neither sought nor knew.
> Some view our sable race with scornful eye,
> "Their colour is a diabolic dye."
> Remember, Christians, Negroes, black as Cain,
> May be refin'd, and join th' angelic train.

Wheatley, while crediting slavery and the Divine for bringing her to Christianity, employs that very Christianity to buttress a subtle argument for a more critical stance on the part of the reader toward slavery, and more obviously, a more favorable understanding of enslaved Africans and African-Americans.

Emma Lazarus, an American poet born of Portuguese Sephardic Jewish parents in New York, also writes America. In her 1883 sonnet, "The New Colossus," she places in the mouth of Liberty the recognizable words, "Give me your tired, your poor, [y]our huddled masses yearning to breathe free." Engraved on a plaque mounted in 1903 at the base of *Liberté éclairant le Monde*—the Statue of Liberty, a gift to the United States from France—the poem transformed sculptor Frédéric Auguste Bartholdi's statue from a symbol of intercontinental republican ideals and liberty to the Mother of exiles, the Mother of new Americans.

Lazarus, Wheatley, and de Crèvecoeur, while participating in the articulation of America, also demonstrate its multiplicity; that which has always marked Americans but presented a threat to the nation's early theorists. The founding Fathers eschewed, at a critical moment in U.S. history, the considerable promise of a multicultural America for a monoculture constructed around Protestant Anglo cultural and political values and aesthetics; assigning freedom, citizenship, and agency to those most closely aligned with them. Any discussion of a national literature is underlain, I believe, with the often-tacit and long-standing tension between what America is and the idea of America.

American poet Langston Hughes, in a poem published in 1935, explores the distance between the American Dream and poor Americans: the poor white, the Negro, the Indian, the immigrant, the farmer, the worker. "Let America Be America Again" unyieldingly holds a mirror up to American inequity. At the same time it does not abandon a national ethos. Conveyed at the poem's very end is the hope for an America that can live up to its expressed principles of democracy, and freedom for all. Through the poem, Hughes unites the aforementioned and various communities and identities within a framework of social justice.

America is best when it recognizes its inherent plurality. Americans are best when, embracing plurality, we move toward and seek to understand those around us. Americans are best when we are engaged and dialogic. Not presuming sameness paradoxically allows us to arrive at shared qualities. It allows us to see that, though different in many ways, de Crèvecoeur, Wheatley, and Lazarus, were each immigrants or the descendants of immigrants. They were bicultural, and bilingual, if not speakers of several languages. Each writer read widely. Each pursued and maintained literary connections in the broad world. Each looked inward to America for a vision of it, and themselves.

In the same spirit, American poetry as a body is best when it reflects America's inherent pluralism and defies the monoculture America never truly was.

I: Self-Definition

Lisboa, Tanga, Goa

Megan Fernandes

> "The historical narrative of Tanga—if one can be said to exist—is sparse, fragmentary, and heavy with silence."
> —Kelly Askew, *Performing the Nation: Swahili Music and Cultural Production in Tanzania*

> "It was the year he began to wonder about the noise that colors make."
> —Anne Carson, *The Autobiography of Red*

First was Serafino, then Alcoque, and a few weeks ago, Januar.

After I returned home from a two-month stint in Lisbon, my uncle died. This was my father's third brother in three years to pass away. It was sudden. He died in the town where he had always lived and where both my parents were born and grew up: in Tanga, Tanzania. I thought to the last time I had seen Januar, a few years ago on a grassy raised beach in Tanga, celebrating my sister's engagement. The land was part of a ruined estate where my cousin, Rosemary, and I sat above a cast iron cauldron, boiled water for chai tea, tugged at the weeds slipping through the wet rocks. This was my first time meeting Rose, Januar's daughter. She was younger than me, already engaged and ready to move to Zanzibar and live with her fiancé and his family. Rose and I got on remarkably well for being strangers, had an odd and immediate intimacy, a warm penchant for sarcasm. A few months later while studying in France, Rose asked if I would come back to Zanzibar for her wedding and be her maid of honor. I thought of Rose writing to me from her narrow, multi-level tree-house apartment in Stonetown, the whole neighborhood smelling of treated wood and brass plates, the ornamentation of Zanzibar's famous wooden artisanal chests. When she asked, I was broke, and knowing I was unable to afford the flight, I felt a terrible guilt. I cried to my boyfriend, who told me calmly in our poorly lit Parisian studio that this was part of diasporic living. Guilt is part of this.

For years, I only read Irish poetry. I was particularly drawn to the Northern Irish female poets, such as Medbh McGuckian (probably, my favorite living poet). McGuckian did strange, riveting things with language. I never looked to poets that talked in a specific or didactic way about diasporic experience. This was too obvious, too "neat," and we don't come to know about our cultural histories neatly, but in a confused, palimpsestic mode of storytelling and error. The key to some "other-wordly" transgressive space was always in the language and syntax, the experimentation with idiom, and the power of surreal, non-representational imagery. I probably read McGuckian's *Captain Lavender* a hundred times, where in states of wildness, she described "flinging" colors, or an "afternoon of staircase," etc. I was moved by not only her freedom with the materiality of language itself, but also with her musicality (which I think is missing in a lot of "language" poetry). From McGuckian, I found myself reading some of the most loquacious work of Jorie Graham, particularly *The Errancy* and Eleni Sikelianos' *Body Clock*. These were the collections, along with some early feminist language theorists such as Kristeva and Cixous, that allowed me to think more bravely about the nuances of language. And eventually, it was not *Beowulf, The*

Iliad, or *Paradise Lost,* but rather, Anne Carson's *The Autobiography of Red* that really started me thinking about the power of epic and the wondrous brazenness of *"in media res."* I think it was because I finally realized that no beginnings were sufficient; there was no way to introduce conflict except to be dropped into the conflict itself. The central problem of diasporic experience was a representational problem. Instead of a clear genealogical history, I felt like a writer who was knit, as Jorie Graham says in her poem "The Guardian Angel of the Little Utopia," of a "crumpled dust."

When somebody makes inquiries about my last name, I tell them that my family is a testament to the incredibly complicated ways in which colonization works. My family are African Goans. They are Portuguese colonized Indians (Goa is the smallest province in India) that were displaced to East Africa (Tanzania) for three generations and lived under British occupation. When people ask, I tell them that my parents feel very differently about this occupation, and that this has perhaps always been a subconscious tension that I experienced while growing up in their household. I tell them that my mother is more Indian, my father more Tanzanian, and that they both speak not only Swahili and English, but my father also speaks Konkani, an Indo-Aryan language that was often referred to as the *lingua canarim* of the Portuguese. The Portuguese (since Vasco de Gama entered India in 1498) brought pork vindaloo and prawn balchao, sweets such as petas de freiras, pasteis de natas to Goan cuisine. My maternal grandfather used to write for the *Times of India* and the *Navhind Times* (Panjim, Goa publication), telling tales of the Portuguese ditties that his brother would recite to outwit his parents. These tales were humorous, but sometimes also painful and humiliating accounts of the cross-generational gaps that occurred in his childhood, in which he was moving between two politically unstable nations: India and Tanzania. This was the same grandfather who, upon hearing that his seven-year-old granddaughter had told her mother she wanted to be white like all the other "American" girls in her class, sent a newspaper clipping of Miss India (who won Miss Universe that year) laminated to a piece of cardboard with a note stating "You should be proud to be Indian."

My experience as an immigrant poet and as a child of parents with such a complex history is to resist a certain politically correct, easy categorization of "diverse" poets. When we marginalize these poets, however good the intentions, we reaffirm the mainstream canon of white, male poets. In my opinion, this kind of multiculturalism is not the heart of diasporic writing. Rather, it is a stutter, an uncertain and inexplicable desire to express something that eludes all systems of representation. What could this complexity look like? Sound like? What kind of experiment could ever possess the sensibility so perfectly constructed as Anne Carson's Geryon, that little winged transgenic red monster who perhaps was not diasporic in the contemporary literal political sense, but who was a creature of "scattered" potential, who wanted to know the noises that colors make when he heard the roses "roaring across the garden towards him"?

Carson's Geryon is a creature obsessed with accidents and imprisonment. He mulls over captured whales, wonders over the spontaneity of volcanic rock, tells his brother that cage is his favorite weapon. In other words, his concerns are so humanist in the face of governing structures of power that in his own way, he teaches us about risk and captivity, humiliation and agency. What results is a newly fashioned sensibility, a way of experiencing that is illogically surreal and fragmented. What does Geryon tell me about diasporic writing? He troubles the very reality that holds his dystopic world in place. He reads about "mood" in Heidegger. He fails often. He is the moody, failing philosopher, and yet, it is his own wavering between epiphany and sorrow that marks the limitations of not him, but his homeland. This is the frustration of every diasporic writer. There is no homeland, no neat patriotism, no singular space of reference. There is only the constant interpretation of what we mean by "culture" or "community," re-writing itself over and over again. Geryon does see a static world, he sees the dynamics of conquest and the uncertainty of the results.

In May of 2012, I left the United States for a two-month writing fellowship in Lisbon, a city with a rich literary history of Indo-Lusophone and Afro-Portuguese literature, and whose current literary community is intent on probing that history. In particular, I was interested in the delayed yet primal modernist moments of 20th century Portuguese literature, when not only Fernando Pessoa, but also writers such as Adeodato Barreto and Francisco José Tenreiro (the editor of *Panorâmica da literatura norte-americana* (1945) and an important anthology of Afro-Portuguese poetry called the *Antologia da Poesia Negra de Expressão Portuguesa*), were reappropriating the "negro" aesthetics of the Harlem Renaissance in a completely new context. I didn't want to make my writing clinical or like a research paper, but I knew that Portugal would provide an important history for me. I was curious about the hybridity of languages, the way in which Portugal, as one of Europe's oldest borders, allowed for a complex political and literary identity to make their way into imagery, tone, and poetic forms. In 2012, and one of the major reasons I wanted to travel to Lisbon, I attended the "Disquiet" Summer Writing Festival, partly funded by the Portuguese government (Center for National Culture) and party funded by Dzanc Books. At "Disquiet," I participated in a "Luso-experience" workshop. The class was cross-genre and cross-generational. Many of the participants were from New Bedford or Provincetown, most of them Azorean and some who could speak fluent Portuguese. Our workshop teacher kept telling us that someone needed to write the great Portuguese-American novel, put Portuguese-American literature on the map, talk about how the largest ethnic population in New England was Portuguese. But this wasn't my experience of being Portuguese, which for me was so far almost untraceable, a diasporic fingerprint on a confusing, fluctuating, and evolving history of colonization and displacement.

In Lisbon, I met for the first time my cousin Jason, a queer Catholic intellectual pursuing his PhD on the citizenship experience of the Goan Catholic at the University of Lisboa. Jason lived in the servant's quarters of a wealthy Portuguese art dealer, and he would take me through the house like a museum curator, explaining the origins and regional value of the rare tapestries, portraits, and ceramics out on display. In particular, he was quite taken with the china cabinet, delighted at how many different sizes of plates and glass soup ladles could exist in one set, the residue of old world luxury. Jason and I argued often. I sympathized with his many contradictions knowing full well that as a sensitive and intelligent person, he kept himself up at night with a healthy amount of inner conflict. But he was a Europhile who was also a postcolonial scholar, someone who saw empire as both productive and oppressive, and it was this simultaneous romanticization and criticism of institutions such as colonization and the church that I found endlessly curious. At a party in Lisbon, when an American artist asked him to speak about his experience of growing up as a gay Indian (to which he specifically pointed out that he was Goan, which was *quite* different), I became angry. Don't romanticize that narrative, I said, maybe unfairly. You're smarter than this, Jason. It's not a sin. He let me be angry, smiled, told me

I was so westernized, I didn't understand, I didn't grow up in Goa, in the small, conservative and religious area around Panjim. *Will you go back?* I had asked. *Yes*, he said. *Yes*, he wanted to go back. *But you can't be yourself there*, I pressed. *Yes, but I am also Goan. Goa is also who I am.* Jason once asked what people think I am in the US, I told him that my response usually falters into a series of incoherent, half-joking digressions:

It's not hispanic, it's Portuguese… Fernandes with an "s", not a "z"… I keep getting my Comcast bills in Spanish… well, I know, that's because I *am* Indian. Well I'm Indian, but really Goan… Hindi? No, not Hindi. Well, my parents were born in East Africa so they speak Swahili… Yes, really… Born and raised Catholics, so sorry my wedding will be as white and boring as yours… Actually, they lived under British occupation so you know, they have Britishisms and say things like "bloody" and "twit"… Yea, but I was born in Canada… Been here about 20 years, and now… Dual citizenship, actually… But I have an American passport…

Jason laughed, told me that this was not so uncommon in Lisbon. There were so many people whose families went through Kenya and Tanzania. I felt unoriginal, and then gross about feeling that way. Sometimes I can't help but exoticize my own narrative, I told him. It feels so foreign to me. He smiled, said it was good to think about these things. They're complicated. There will always be more at stake in Goa for you than for me, I said. I am not sure where my stakes are yet.

As I wandered Lisbon that summer, particularly the botanical garden at the University of Lisboa in the Principe Real neighborhood of the city, I found myself writing lines about the "quaking aspen" and the "yellow ballerina vines" of trees. The poems all ended, though, with either a primal scene from my childhood in

Canada or a question of language and translation. I thought to myself, why do I continue to arrive at these two movements? These are not unusual subjects for poets, but to me, they felt indicative of something unusually sentimental for my taste. I thought of the early poems of Yeats, a corpus I knew well and that many esteemed poets told me I would grow to see as juvenile compared to his masterpieces written later in his life. But I think what appealed to me (and what still appeals to me) is that earnest, romantic Yeats was so dedicated in parsing Celtic mythology, in establishing a historical and literary identity though his political ideas wavered. The more I wrote that summer, when thinking so structurally about the politics of diaspora, the more I became drunk with nonsensical, whimsical lines. I found myself pacing uphill through the city's seven peaks repeating a verse from Yeats' "Brown Penny":

'Go and love, go and love, young man,
If the lady be young and fair.'
Ah, penny, brown penny, brown penny,
I am looped in the loops of her hair.

Harness

Sun Yung Shin

Facts

I am a flesh ghost.
입 양 인 임 니 다. *Ibyangin imnida.*
[*bowing*]
I am an "adoptee."
만마서 반갑습니다. *Mannaseo pangapsumnida.*
It's nice to meet you.
How should I address you?

To Say

"... the Korean language strictly reflects the
hierarchical order. Speech styles are divided
according to a system of honorifics, and this
system is complex and richly textured. In fact,
it may well be that no language on earth has a
more finely differentiated system of honorifics."[1]

Drown

I dance in a *bi-archy*. The person I left behind.
The Korean woman with a Korean life. Who
writes in Korean not English. An order of
intimate estrangement.

We meet sometimes. At night. When bending
over a simple plate of water. In dreams, when

passing through the gates, going opposite
directions, into the past, into the future.

The gorgeous, drowned oneirautics.

My doppelganger speaks in tongues. Moves
when I move, drinks black air with my wine, fills
and fills.

She clings to my back and whispers in my ear.
We have our own language. She curses me, she
pulls my hair, she is afraid of water.

What   *Korean, unborn, [name], abandoned, orphan,
           [named], foster child, [renamed], adoptee,
           immigrant, legal alien, naturalized citizen, [return
           to the second name], member of the diaspora,
           potentially eligible for dual citizenship, ashes to
           ashes…*

Water   I am a graveyard of names.
           They pile up like cards in a baby-sized box.
           The box soaks and swells.
           Leaks and bursts, a balloon, a boat, a floating
           thing.

Blanks   I may be named after a police station: Shin-Kyo
           Police Box, which may have originally been one
           of the many Japanese police stations built during
           the occupation era. The Hermit Kingdom pried
           open like an oyster.

Invasions	Mongols (1231)
	Japanese (1592)
	Manchus (1627)

Japan[2]   Three stages of the Japanese Colonial Era:

- "the dark age of" <u>Subjugation</u> (1910–1919) "where the military ruled by threat and violence"
- <u>Cultural accommodation</u> (1920–1931) "after the Korean Independence Movement in March 1919" "allowing some freedom in schools, newspapers, and businesses"
- <u>Assimilation</u> (1931–1945) "renewed tightening of controls and forced participation in the Japanese war effort"

Ur-Father   I was born thirteen years after 박 정 희 Park Chung-hee seized power in a coup d'état and two years after he declared military rule and declared himself President for Life. Three months and two days after my (paper) birthday, there was an assassination attempt. The killer missed him but a stray bullet hit his wife. Later that day, she died.

Documented   Abandoned at 9 p.m. on January 20, 1975, at the Holt Office in Seoul, Korea. Processed at the Shin-Kyo Police Station.

신 *(Shin)*   Knocked loose.

Family of one.

At seven months old, I become the Chief and sole member of (my new branch of) the Shin family.

"Shin is a Korean family name. It is cognate to the Chinese family names Shen and Xin. According to the 2000 census in South Korea, there were 911,556 people carrying the Shin surname."[3]

"No Record" Orphan 호적 (hojuk). In her article "Our Adoptee, Our Alien: Transnational Adoptees as Specters of Family and Foreignness in Korea," Eleana Kim explains how the "orphan hojuk" and the legal orphanization (my term) process reconstitutes the adoptee socially in Korea. Within "the context of Korean law, she becomes a person with the barest of social identities, and in the context of Korean cultural norms, she lacks the basic requirements of social personhood—namely, family lineage and genealogical history."[4]

Below are two images, both copies, of my "orphan hojuk," or the family registry created so that I could be separated legally from my (anonymous) Korean family and made available for intercountry adoption. The first is an English translation of the second. What I have is a hasty and terrible photocopy, dark and illegible, the Korean original. Yet, an original of what?

My existence is, among other things, a kind of
deformation, a defamation in my home country.
An ill report, rumor, scandal. A secret.
I am a copy and an original.
I will make a record.

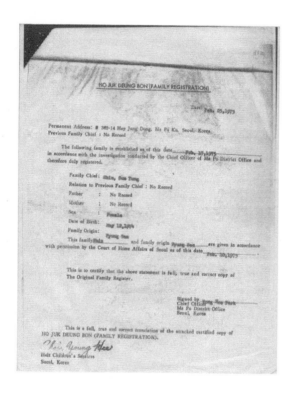

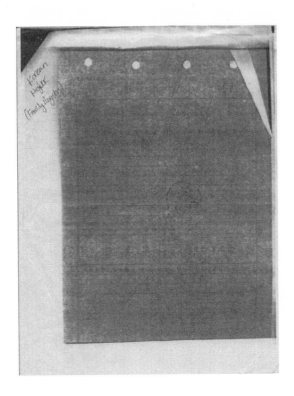

In these copies, light escapes at the corners.

Sudden   I am a colony of one.[5]

Though the καταστροφῶν, *katastrofón*,
catastrophes of war were over, mothers were still
compelled to ~~eat~~ send their children far across
the sea.

καταστροφή. *An overturning. To turn down. To*
trample on. A sudden end.

Ride

I walk through the dark forest and out beyond to steal the fire from the skulls for my stepmother. My mother dead, her gift of a magic talking doll deep in my trembling pocket. The enigmatic Russian folktale of Beautiful Vassilisa.

All day she walked on. Towards evening she came to a glade. She looked into the glade and saw a hut; all round it was a fence made from human bones. On the fence were human skulls; human legbones served instead of a gate, there were hands instead of bolts, and sharp teeth acted as the lock. At this sight the girl was terrified: she stood rooted to the ground. Suddenly a horseman rode past; he was dressed entirely in black, was riding a black horse, and the horse's harness, too, was black. He galloped up to the gate and vanished as if he had been swallowed into the earth. Night came on.[6]

To beg > borrow > burn.
A coup d'état of this, my abandonment, my miniature καταστροφή!

To write this *immigration* as it comes on and on like black Night on its black horse. These pages my glade and my harness.

Notes

1. Lee, Iksop and S. Robert Ramsey, "Chapter 7: Honorifics and Speech Styles," *The Korean Language*. Albany, NY: State University of New York Press, 2000. p 224.

2. Kang, Hildi. "Introduction," *Under the Black Umbrella: Voices from Colonial Korea*. NY: Cornell University, 2001. p 2.

3. http://en.wikipedia.org/wiki/Shin_(Korean_name).

4. Kim, Eleana, *Anthropological Quarterly*. Spring 2007, Vol. 80 Issue 2, p 497–531. 35p.

5. Credit for the idea of a Korean adoptee as a "colony of one" goes to Kim Park Nelson.

6. "Beautiful Vassilisa," http://www.artrusse.ca/fairytales/vassilisa.htm.

Snowflake Falling Through Time
A Bengali-American Story
Zubair Ahmed

I began finding myself as a poet when I stopped thinking in Bengali and switched to thinking in English. This switch happened in 2005, when I immigrated to America with my parents as a sixteen-year-old. Over the following years, I went through cycles of struggle, recovery, and enlightenment. Particularly from 2011 to 2013, I suffered and reinvented myself.

My story emerges from stitching these cycles together, and I view my past as a collection of stories. Each story is a unique thread in the clothes of my life. Each story, along with my thoughts, feelings, and actions within that story, influences and gives rise to my poetry.

In my journey after leaving Bangladesh, I found bits and pieces of what it means to be a poet. For me, what defines a poet is how the poet eludes definition. A poet is a consequence of loving language. A poet gives meaning to existence, and gives existence to meaning. A poet is a wanderer. A poet is both hunger and thirst. A poet is a snowflake falling through time, a design that may or may not be studied.

I'm grateful to be an immigrant. Without any say in the matter, I was handed a perspective I had to understand to feel alive—the perspective of the outsider in a place he cannot leave. Faced with uncertainty, I found my balance by listening to people, by observing how they behave, and by building an understanding of their culture. In this process, I fell in love with English language. Somewhere along the way, I began writing poetry. Given my fortune and outlook, near the end of 2013, I found a home in Seattle, Washington, as an engineer at Boeing.

Through this fortune, I'm humbled to have found some pieces of myself. When I shifted cultures in 2005, I unhooked the doors for my insatiable curiosity, which began flowing like water into all the corners of my imagination, where it inevitably found the wreckages and burnt landscapes left behind by my insecurities and my displacement from home. Eventually, thanks to chance friendships and enlightenments, this water washed away all but the core I now cherish as my soul, which is my only unchanging component. I've found my center—a man with his tools in this world. With these tools, I'm crafting my identity in America, where I believe the free mind can still forge original ideas into existence. I'm building inside and outside my body. I'm putting together the roadmap of my happiness. But reaching this point was difficult for me.

I found extraordinary friction where my natural tendencies met with unknown cultural and societal expectations. This friction generated sparks, causing many fires I've had to extinguish, and many I've abandoned to the ruins of time. I burned in these flames. I felt my flesh being stretched on my bones by their light. I made food above these flames. Their heat put me to sleep. Several times, I crawled out of my skin because I hoped to change my mistakes. I searched for a sense of belonging, comfort, and peace. For eight years, I tried to become a new man. Each time the new man I became held his new doubts, and the circle continued until it ended the moment I graduated in June 2013.

The previous year and a half were particularly challenging for me. During 2012, for the first time in my life, I considered suicide. Overloaded with expectations and facing overwhelming uncertainty in my responsibilities, I didn't know what to do. I became numb and emotionless. I could barely keep up with my research and schoolwork. I stopped eating regularly. I became desperate roaming in my own darkness.

But I held on to the light thanks to a sentence whispered by my father as he lay on his stretcher, heading to the operating room after a severe heart attack in 2010. Five of his arteries were clogged. He touched my wrist and said, "It's not my time yet." I drew strength from him. And so, I began my search for recovery.

During this search, in January 2013, I stumbled onto Ithaka, a community of intellectuals, hippies, and philosophers living in the middle of Palo Alto, California. Most people here were students or former students of Stanford University, but it wasn't an exclusive space. Notably, an MMA fighter and his massage therapist brother added to the diversity of lifestyles. Together, we maintained a few houses, grew food in our gardens, and gave business to our local farms. We respected each other. We believed in the future, in everything good and kind. We lived in a way that gave me life.

But during my recovery, I was dealt a blow. In March 2013, a group of housemates, friends, and I set off for a five-day adventure in the Grand Canyon. We would hike deep into the canyon, and I was excited! I had never been on such a journey, and my curiosity got me ready for a memorable experience. As our engines revved through the Arizona desert, I received a call informing me that my best friend had gone into a coma that morning, during routine wisdom teeth extraction. By the time I came back from my trip, he was dead at only 24 years old.

Even though I'm not a stranger to death, I was shaken and lost. Moreover, with pressing graduation deadlines, I had no time to mourn. Under pressure of reconstructing my still recovering mind, under pressure of finishing my studies, I had no option but to move forward—it's what my friend would have wanted. I bottled my emotions for a few poems. Remembering our words, committing to our plans, I made vows to pursue and accomplish our shared dreams.

Bracing in for the ride with pursed lips, I gathered strength for a final push through my last few months as a student. I drew on the joys of the beautiful life I had found in Ithaka. I gave my prayers, remembered past lessons, and allowed time to flow her water through me. My reward came on June 16, 2013, the moment I walked down from the stage at Stanford University with my B.S. and M.S. degrees, a first generation graduate. I had reached an end! Unknowingly, I had also found a beginning.

In what seemed to be a quantum of a moment, old gears began shedding their dust inside me. They began oiling their bearings, and moving the neglected machine I now know as my Bangladeshi identity. This machine rose up between my bones to say goodbye. To say, America is your home. This machine imbued my suffering with meaning, revitalized my flesh, and poured water over the wound left by my departed friend. This machine gave me clarity, then disappeared.

So in the moment I finished my education, I unified my identity as a Bengali-American and no longer a Bangladeshi in America. I reinvented myself. I began unchaining my past from my skin. I felt wild, sophisticated, and alive! Ready for a future filled with change. And importantly, I found time to mourn. To recover, and reflect. To let this thread of my life story sit inside me, and give rise to poetry.

Why I Am (Not) an Immigrant Poet

Anis Shivani

It's intriguing but until I was asked to contribute to this anthology it had never once occurred to me to think of myself as an immigrant poet. Or to think of myself as an immigrant writer, period, since I also write in other genres. So I'll have to go about addressing this issue negatively, wondering why not, rather than explaining why something is so, and hope to learn something about myself as I gather my thoughts.

An immigrant poet would obviously be someone whose identity as an immigrant is important to him or her. The country of origin remains part of the imaginary landscape, whether in nostalgia, sentimentality, anger, bitterness, appreciation, or condemnation. I know many poets like that (and I may even be one myself). There is constant metaphysical back and forth, as though one were straddling fences, remembering the old, glamorizing the new, trying to forget trauma and pain and loss, advocating for impossible love and fulfillment and completion. Much is gained when one hovers over two worlds, acts as though one is not a citizen of either, assumes statelessness in the literary realm, a fantasy condition without resolution. It can provide solace.

But in fact one is always a citizen of one or another world. Perhaps for a time a semblance of in-betweenness can be maintained. A probationary period, a trial balloon. A time of adopting new exteriors, shedding old skins, discarding unnecessary baggage. But after that, resolution and commitment have to follow. One ends up becoming place-bound, geographically determined.

But the immigrant poet can choose to adopt the (im)posture indefinitely, make the undecidability the basis of his or her poetry. Why let go of a convenient pain, which is actually a position of privilege? To adopt the persona of the immigrant poet—a mark of distinction, something to separate oneself from the thousands of poets operating today in America—eases the path, provides an avenue of niche marketability in a time of ferocious literary competition.

The immigrant poet can get away with a lot. If she is to valorize China before the communist revolution or the paradise of Andalus under Muslim rule who is to question her? Likewise if she is to condemn China during the cultural revolution or Iran under the ayatollahs who is to question her? The immigrant poet is allowed to skate history, or rather, choose to withhold it if necessary, because her pain of emigration is supposed to make us cut her some slack. We take her word for what she tells us about the other world. It's even better if that world happens to match the journalistically created worlds we consume like beer or pizza.

But as I said, one is always a citizen of a particular world. The immigrant poet is not the poet of exile. Or if he or she is, then I become interested. There is a qualitative difference between a poet who is raised in the U.S., goes to school here and participates in all of popular culture's fantasies and convictions, versus someone forced to be an emigrant, an exile rather, someone of the mold of Joseph Brodsky or perhaps the Russian diaspora in Western Europe in the

1920s and 1930s. One is a pose, the other is a necessity. I choose to live in the world of necessity.

The immigrant poet seeks to defer the question of allegiance and this is attractive to certain sensibilities, but the deferment of allegiance has never appealed to me, perhaps because I'm what's known in therapeutic lingo as "judgmental." I originally come from Pakistan, so technically I'm an immigrant. I emigrated to a place of more freedom, leaving cultural baggage behind, never looked back. Looking back, I was afraid, might kill me. Indeed, whenever I've tried to look back, it hasn't been good. I don't fit where I came from, and I marvel at those who leave their countries of origin behind, are for all intents and purposes citizens of a place that has nothing in common with the place they left, yet they pick and choose from it things to like and dislike. I'm sorry but I have too judgmental a character to menu-pick like that.

I don't even know what the Pakistani or Indian or South Asian poetic tradition is, really. What little I know of it doesn't suit my modernist sensibility. I may know a little about Ghalib, but I don't respond to him, nor do I have any emotional or intellectual response to any of the other great Urdu poets I'm vaguely familiar with. They write in a flowery, romantic vein, are premodern in the sense that the weight of the last two centuries' ills and traumas, and yes pleasures, hasn't hit them. To me it's an alien world, a way of thinking that's not part of my mental apparatus. I see a love-hate relationship with the West in that writing, hypocrisy and delusion, and it doesn't appeal to me—it's not even relevant to me. It's a feudal world.

I'm afraid of romanticizing, of being untrue, of not being faithful to necessity. I dislike the word pragmatic, and have often censured it, but perhaps I'm pragmatic in my self-conception as an author, and not pragmatic in my writing. That may be one way of describing the lack of division I feel within myself. I refuse to divide myself in ways that feel untrue.

The lack of emotional response doesn't hold when I look at ancient Chinese poetry, which, in its focus on the image, or economy of words, or allusiveness and silence, seems damned modern to me. I respond to it very deeply, it's a world that doesn't feel alien to me.

But this is not how I entered the poetry portal. For me the British romantics came first, at a very young age, though once I became adult their appeal faded quickly. I can still derive pleasure from Wordsworth's *Prelude* and much of Shelley, but the modernists are where I settled early on and I'm still there. Eliot and Stevens and Pound were the biggest influences. Lately I've been rereading Stevens for his playfulness, especially *Harmonium*. I love all the modernists, they are my lodestone, because they took on the challenge of imposing their forceful imagination on a world spinning out of control, because they refused to accept the defeat of literature in a time of mass conformity and delusion. I love all those who have explored the bounds of language, from Olson and Oppen to Berryman and Berrigan to Zukofsky and Duncan. I love the New York School, all the waves within it, and I'm consumed by Frank O'Hara and Kenneth Koch and Bernadette Meyer. I've recently become fond of flarf and conceptual poetry. I'll take quirky e.e. cummings's humor any day over the depressive confessionalists screaming for my attention.

I think what's common to all the poetry I love is a sense of playfulness rather than obligatory earnestness, a focus on language rather than meaning (meaning ensues from language, I think, not the other way around). There's a division these days in American poetry between lyric poetry—which wins most of the awards, is the poetry primarily published by major publishing houses like Norton and Knopf, and is the only recognizable mainstream poetry—and language poetry and its descendants, which thrive in certain writing programs, have their own culture within the poetry world, and think of themselves as avant-garde, even though much of the impulse has been thoroughly canonized, even cannibalized, for decades now.

As an immigrant—or not-immigrant—poet, neither tendency satisfies me, and I'd say that my poetry tries to bridge the two. Lyric poetry is too little focused on play of language to gratify me. I think of immigrant poetry today as a subset of confessionalist poetics. The immigrant poet qua immigrant poet confesses how he or she fits or doesn't fit, how he or she belongs or doesn't belong, how he or she misses or doesn't miss the old country. Confessionalism doesn't do it for me, earnestness doesn't either. As for language poetry and its various offshoots, they are too uninterested in meaning. Of course, this is explicitly their agenda, because meaning proceeding according to bourgeois construction of sentences and logic is suspect, all but fascist. (This is the pragmatic immigrant in me coming out, is it not?)

If I had to choose, I would undoubtedly go with experimental poetry, since it at least takes the first step of prioritizing language. Are "immigrant poets" experimentalist? Typically not. (Or am I wrong?) What I try to do in my poetry is be experimental—difficult, modernist, challenging—at the same time as I reach for a scaffold of meaning. I don't need to be didactic, but I can't let it go at the idea that it's fun enough to see how words assembled on paper construct their own meaning. They always do, of course, but there has to be a little something beyond that.

When I look at the poetry I actually write, however, it seems to me that I must be an immigrant poet par excellence. Just not in the way we think of immigrant poets, who write solemn, nostalgic, identity-asserting, schizophrenia-overcoming poems, crooning about mangoes and rivers and places of worship in their home countries (which aren't really their homes) even as they shop at Whole Foods and self-promote on Facebook or whatever it is that poets do when they're not being poets.

But the immigrant as voice of justice—because he or she is presumably more sensitive to injustice than the native population—is something very powerful I respond to. Many of the modernist American poets I love have been Jewish, and a lot of their idealism (or stubbornness) comes through in my poetry as well.

I'm looking at some of my newest poems at random to see what stands out with respect to the issue of the immigrant poet. There is a long collage poem on E.M. Forster's gay loves in post-World War I Alexandria. Exile upon exile upon exile. This interests me very much. There are levels of illicitness, something the immigrant always struggles with, no matter how adept or shapeshifting or incorporated he becomes.

There are my "Sonnets to X.," one of which ends: "I read all the books worth reading in the womb. / An immigrant is an explosion waiting to happen. / You want me to count the ways I love you? / Fraulein X., I am black chalk in a Berlin cave." One reading of these sonnets would be that it is an immigrant's lament for the things he can never have, because he is an immigrant, because he is in the condition of knowing too much to enjoy pleasures naively like the native-born.

I have a found poem about the Beats, a stanza of which reads: "his wild eye, a 'real' American, sucked such a poem right / out of America, with that little camera he raises and snaps with / one hand, the crazy feeling in America, the result is America." This seems to crystallize a lot of my persistent themes. Protest against an America that usually fails to live up to (the immigrant's) high expectations, desire to opt out of the crude materialism/consumerism to which most writers/intellectuals seem to have succumbed in their university professionalism, a great big Fuck You and Damn You, expressed in the most loving manner possible, of course. Ginsberg was very good at that, so he remains an idol. Immigrants are less likely to have thoughts such as "It's okay for them to read your email or tap your phones if you have nothing to hide" or give in to the claptrap about "existential" threats compelling us to give up our freedoms, so that we choose to live in prison because we're afraid to live in prison.

There's another new poem called "Poets," one of many that I like to write about the process of poetry, another found poem, which begins: "i don't mean to presume uh every boy needs / poets in dream oboeland, oh my syrian robes." The first line is borrowed from Ron Silliman. I think this poem's attitude toward how poetry comes about is typical of me. An immigrant is nothing if he doesn't screw up the orderly ways of thinking for the native establishment. Poetry works the same way with the orders of language.

Another new poem is called "Between the Wars" and it extracts first from *A Farewell to Arms* and then from *Tropic of Cancer* to illustrate the different yet similar attitudes Hemingway and Henry Miller felt toward interwar Europe, especially when it came to sexuality. Both exiles, both uncomfortable in their skins, emigrants from the land of the free and the home of the brave, desperate to escape provinciality and finding it in Paris and other European capitals of the time, and both achingly relevant to today when the emigrant has nowhere to escape, when the whole world has been colonized by vulgar capitalism.

My book *My Tranquil War and Other Poems* (NYQ Books, 2012) has similar tendencies, very marked at that. These poems were written over the course of the Bush years, the most anti-immigrant period in American history since at least the 1920s. Many writers, faced with the assault, retreated further into the safe multicultural/ academic cocoon. I, for one, lost my naïve patriotism, which I used to possess in great quantities before the (now thankfully concluded) fascist episode of the last decade. My poetry was deeply affected, though now I've reached a point of resignation toward America, the whole project, that lets me go on without soaking in the bad news. I've learned to deflect and parry and ignore, not that the assaults on privacy and autonomy and liberty are any less severe.

In my book there are many poems rooted in the anxieties of post-9/11 America, for instance one about Salman Rushdie being frisked and detained, another called "Dear President Bush," a long poem addressing Walt Whitman and wondering what he would think of the collapse of the American ideal, and many poems informed by the madness of war. In fact, one of the five sections of the book is titled "War," and here, in a poem like "Remembering Manzanar," are all the stresses of the immigrant reflected back to an uncomprehending native population—because they have nothing to hide, so why should they worry?

This book of mine seems resolved to fight the attitude of the time, the "us versus them" impulse. I think the worst thing a poet can do in such a time is to buy into official categories—which many did by the act of defining themselves, more fancifully and imaginatively, precisely as the fascist authorities would have liked, as the beloved/ haunted other. Fascism trickled deep down into society, especially in writing and academics. It impacted everyone. The only refuge in such a time, for any poet, is to carve out an autonomous space for art. This in the end is what prevents so-called "political poetry" from being didactic.

Toward the end of the decade, we elected a messiah—with a bit of a pretense himself about writing poetry—and as an immigrant (by this point in the essay I'm loose enough to identify myself with this label) I remained wary, where so many other poets, immigrant or not, bent under the weight of a guilt that could not be faced, a shame that could not be confronted, and wrote as though the body politic had been cleansed. It remains filthy as ever. So filthy that I choose mostly not to write about it anymore. It distorts me as a poet, but I don't know what else to do.

So yes, I am an immigrant poet, in all the ways it counts. I just don't want to be thought of as solemn and earnest. I don't want to be identified with any group. I refute the false equivalency of poetic traditions. What is mine has come to me through blood, sweat, and tears, and I won't let anyone take it away from me, though the culture tries hard, wants to make a product and brand out of me, but I won't let it.

Don't you think of yourself as nomadic, I was asked recently? I'm not sure about this term, I prefer cosmopolitan. It's true that after the last decade of forced patriotism, which pushed people like me away from patriotism, I don't feel allegiance to any particular place like I used to before. I'm more loyal to infrastructure (the infrastructure of cultural production) than any specific location, which is a sea change for me.

It's hard to reconcile a poetry of immigration in conditions of nomadic/cosmopolitan rootlessness. It forces me to set my fiction, and often my poetry, in places as far away from the U.S. as possible, places I can idealize and/or deconstruct in a way that the U.S. has lately become resistant to. Ottoman Turkey (completed story). Post-communist Russia (planned novella). Fascist Italy (novel in progress). We went through a decade of incipient fascism in this country, and one way I've dealt with that is by wanting to write a novel of internal exile. (Mussolini had a system of sending dissidents to remote locations within the country.) I suspect medieval settings loom ahead for me in the near future.

I was also asked recently to think about the fact that the theme of immigration occurs differently in my criticism, fiction, and poetry. In criticism my major perspective is world literature, as articulated by Goethe, and later the great comparativists of the interwar years. What qualifies as world literature today, what is worthy of being included, versus what is merely artificial and inorganic, the glossy product of New York and London publishing? So much of immigrant writing in fiction fails to meet, for me, the standards of world literature. So I consciously rebel against that kind of writing, the standard tropes that find acceptance in the genre.

In my fiction immigration has been a dominant—if not the dominant—feature. The fictions in *Anatolia and Other Stories* (Black Lawrence Press, 2009) are often about immigration, or more generally, exile or outsiderness. There is a story, for instance, about a Hungarian gypsy family in 1950s Indiana. There is the opening story of the undocumented Indian worker in modern Dubai. There is the story of the reticent male Issei internee in the Manzanar camp in the early 1940s. I would like to be judged by the fact that I haven't deployed any of the familiar tropes of immigrant fiction, wherein the immigrant suffers from culture shock, gradually adjusts and assimilates, and looks to a brighter future. Something of that narrative is the fallback option, and I refuse to take part in the big lie.

For me immigration is about dismantled yet stubborn psychic processes that are a severe challenge to writers, and the easy way out is to paint over real differences and disjointments. The psychic discomfort, perpetual alienation and self-refutation, probably manifests itself most clearly in my poetry. So perhaps my creative output is split into three parts, each relatively autonomous—though of course feeding on each other—and each deals with immigration in somewhat different ways.

Had I only been a poet, I think I would have been a harsher one, less playful, when it comes to immigration. But I have other outlets. I might well have a blind spot about all this. A huge blind spot. As I reread what I've written so far I realize there's no mention of *The Fifth Lash and Other* Stories (C&R Press, 2012) and my novel, *Karachi Raj*, the labor of many years, which will be published this year. *The Fifth Lash* is mostly about South Asian immigrants, including a story about a stuck-up Middle Eastern Studies professor at Mount Holyoke College, a New York art history student whose husband from an arranged marriage turns out to be wiser than she thought, and a prosperous family in Southern California haunted by the suspicion aimed at Muslims in the wake of 9/11. How could I have "forgotten" to mention this?

Karachi Raj is set in a slum, and is about two ambitious young people trying to escape that orbit. Though not a book of immigration, it is a response in part to that condition. Who am I addressing with that book? It recreates, not always realistically, a lost world and also a world that has not yet come into being, in addition to a sordid world I wouldn't want to be part of. It's an immigrant's recollections (most of them imaginary) of a place of origin that is so far from experience that it affords freedom to imagine. It's an opening as well as a closure, and it's all very complicated because of the problem of audience.

It may well be that I don't want to acknowledge what's closest to myself, the part I "left behind," in order to somehow make myself whole. In a world that acts as though there are no more breaches left, as though all the wounds have been closed and sutured, I'm trying to create new fissures that hurt me the most and yet are tranquilizing.

I think the immigrant writer always operates with a mix of guilt and shame—and pride, which might sometimes be unjustified. Every immigrant writer's work is distorted by these psychological factors. Privilege, is it earned or unearned, survival, can one ever forget its harsh pain, denial, how far can one take it? No doubt I suffer from these disabilities to a greater extent than I know, but my guess is that the work is better because of lack of full awareness. Sometimes it's better not to know that you don't know.

I do know that the world I live in is globalized like never before. People don't emigrate in the old sense they used to, cutting off ties from their original homelands. Modern communications obviate that necessity. Yet the literary world generally prefers narratives of immigration based on the older model. One of the ideas I've begun to articulate is what I call the emerging "global novel," something that seems to me to far exceed the aspirations of the novel of immigration. I hadn't thought about it in connection with poetry, but a global poetry would likewise seek to speak to readers of the future, or of an indeterminate world, rather than specific local audiences (or rather the bosses of the publishing industry and the heads of award committees, who seem to be the real audience).

I ask myself what a global poetry, rather than a poetry of immigration (which suggests movement from A to B, rather than a circular loop from nowhere to nowhere), would look like? By definition it wouldn't be local. I don't want to write as an immigrant poet who's given in to the lures of the local, the regional, the specific, the at-hand and immediately perceptible and respectable. That to me seems a great betrayal of the possibilities of poetry in a global world.

I think the poet in America today is free, freer perhaps than any other artist, because his art is the least acknowledged, the least admired, the least respected. No one knows what we do or why we do it—at least no one outside the community of poets—so we're safe in that respect. This offers untold opportunities. The important thing for me is not to ally with any clique, remain independent, and evolve naturally. Teaching is the great seduction these days, and to the extent that public acclaim and alliances accrue, it dilutes the risks of poetry. Poetry ought to be the most dangerous of arts. Assimilated into the academy, and commercialized structures of language, it loses that.

I have never taught and I never will. I have nothing to teach, least of all to those eager to breathe the rare air of the humanities and the liberal arts. I can only teach annihilation and negation and that is not something anyone would ever pay me to do. I want poetry to come to the untaught.

I see the work of the poet in America today as refuting the baseness to which language has been brought, in the articulations of the academy and politics and popular culture. Language has been utterly trashed. Certain kinds of poetry—the great majority of poetry—collaborates in the trashing of language because it takes the new age tropes of relationships and awareness and wisdom for granted. I think I can honestly say that none of my poems ends in an epiphany. I think what it means to be a poet in America today is to pursue radical uncertainty, put language under a microscope, distort and bend it, set oneself up as a one-man revolutionary band, until every trace of those who set identities and categories ceases to matter.

Poetry should be beautiful, it should give pleasure above all. I've learned not to think beyond myself and my needs. The paradox is that poetry is beautiful only in certain hideouts of egotism. Poets in America today are in a candy store where everything is being given away for free. To make art under such conditions is both the most difficult and the easiest thing. The important thing is to lose one's identity, not hold on to officially approved scraps of it, in whatever version is the flavor of the month, and I do this by seeking rapport with the poets of the past who played with danger and death. I abhor safety. It makes me a despicable immigrant, I know, but I can't have it any other way.

And here, as I open my book again at random, these lines confront me as the opening of "To Robert Creeley": "Creeley, I'm an / immigrant." And later, "Creeley, I / have to settle my accounts, / I thrive on excess." I am seeking permission from Creeley to let me write in a mode of jeopardy whose full extent I cannot allow myself to be aware of or else I would choose silence.

I think all of this reflects anxiety on my part about biography as an appendage to writing, a marketing tool, a qualifying mechanism, a screen, a not-blank canvas where the leftover emotions from poetry are inscribed for public consumption. It makes me uncomfortable. Immigrant poetry seems one more genre where the author is being forced to adopt a precise (romanticized but also resume-oriented) identity, an escape route from the poverty of literary culture. The immigrant poet is encouraged to glorify himself even as the idea he belongs to is collapsing all around him. It's very patronizing, but we fall for it. Biography, in this calculus, becomes a means of self-exorcism, and waves of fear go through me when I think of it like that.

I think poets should make up biographies from whole cloth. But that would mean every poet would have multiple biographies, not just one, and that would scare the hell out of readers, wouldn't it? Besides, in the age of social media, what poet wants to take that risk?

Gatekeepers and Gatecrashers in Contemporary American Poetry
Reflections of a Filipino Immigrant Poet in the United States
Maria Victoria A. Grageda-Smith

Black Lawrence Press' call for essay submissions to the anthology, *Others Will Enter the Gates,* couldn't have come at a better time. I had just reviewed the final draft of my first book of poems entitled, *Warrior Heart, Pilgrim Soul: An Immigrant's Journey,* and the challenge stared me in the eye: Who in United States publishing can possibly be interested in sponsoring the poetry collection of an immigrant poet who, although having achieved success in publishing individual poems, was still relatively unknown (and therefore, perceived to be unbankable)? Was the general American reading public, already largely seen as non-poetry book buyers, ready for a collection of immigrant poetry markedly different in voice, theme, and style from mainstream American poetry?

These questions inevitably led me to a two-pronged query: What is "American" poetry, and what does it mean to be an "American" poet? Since these were the anthology's core areas of interest, I was only too happy to answer the call for submissions, if only as an exercise in exploring my own questions about who I am and where I am going as a writer in the United States.

As in all big questions, I found I had to start from the beginning. And my beginning was this: Like my native country and people, I am, as my poem "A Letter to My Mother"[1] describes,

> ... *Always seemingly caught between worlds—*
> *neither here nor there, neither this nor that,*
> *eluding tidy description, belonging nowhere ...*

I was astounded to realize I was no different, after all, from the riddle within a riddle of a poem I'd long rebelled against.

The core question, "Who is the American poet?" goes into the heart of my writer's identity. Who am I as a writer in the United States? Do I see myself as a Filipino writer who only happens to reside in America? Or do I consider myself an American writer who incidentally has Philippine roots? Does the place in which I write influence what I write, and if so, how does this affect my identity as a writer? So many questions; so many layers of nuanced issues to explore!

For starters, I know that the mere fact I now write solely in English is, in itself, enough for some of my fellow writers in the Philippines to repudiate me as an authentic Filipino writer. To them, language is the medium of identity and failure to write in one's native language is an affront to the culture, betraying the writer as just another neocolonial agent.

Well then, am I simply an American writer who happens to have Philippine heritage? While I am now an American citizen, I suspect this isn't enough to validate me as an "American" writer. I came to the United States at a later age, already immersed in the traditions that shaped and inspired the literature of my native land. My muses are as eclectic as the nationalities of some of the great writers. In poetry, I am especially drawn to literary traditions that derive from the transcendence and humanity of Filipino Dr. José Rizal, American Walt Whitman, and Chilean Pablo Neruda; the contemporary voices of Ted Kooser, Billy Collins, and Charles Wright; the timelessness of William Butler Yeats and T.S. Eliot; the romantic effluence of Emily Dickinson, Elizabeth Barrett Browning, and Edna St. Vincent Millay; the lyrical affluence of Persian poets Omar Khayyám and Melvana Jalal ad-Din Muhammad Rumi, and of Lebanese American Khalil Gibran; the bold sensuality of the ancient Biblical psalmists; and last, but not least, the refreshing child-like innocence, honesty, and elegant simplicity of Theodor Seuss Geisel, fondly known as Dr. Seuss. I try to cull these varied voices together to work and blend them in assisting me to achieve a multicultural, yet universal literary style. I fear, however, that these diverse literary influences, far from helping me to be seen as an "American" poet, in fact, set me apart—thus begging the question, "*Who is* the 'American' poet?"

Is "being" an American writer a function of "place," of where we live and do the act of writing? Or is our identity determined by nationality roots, the dominant socio-cultural construct that thereby becomes the frame of reference for our work? And if that framework is a combination of various socio-cultural perspectives that in my case, for instance, can be seen within the larger context of being Asian, can I identify myself then as an Asian American writer? Many Asians would balk, however, at the categorization of Filipinos as "Asian," and they would not entirely be incorrect, for our cultural world-view compared to that of our neighbors in Southeast Asia is uniquely Western-oriented owing to three hundred and fifty years of Spanish colonial rule and fifty years of American occupation that saw my grandparents become Spanish-speaking Catholics and my parents educated in English-writing-and-speaking classrooms. I was born and raised in a nationalist period in which self-styled patriots proudly embarked upon and announced the creation of a Philippine "national" language they called "Filipino" that later struck me as pretentious because this language turned out to be nothing more than Tagalog, the dialect of the capital city of the largest island in the country, an archipelago composed of more than seven thousand islands with their own regional dialects. Imposing the dialect of the nation's capital on the other regions of the country that have had strong linguistic traditions of their own can be seen as nothing more than the perpetuation of the colonial model earlier denounced by the so-called nationalists before it was re-adopted by them as the now new elite ruling class that forced its own cultural parameters on the ruled. This issue deserves its own essay in another anthology, I'm afraid.

To return to my earlier point: I grew up trilingual, speaking and writing mainly in the two official languages of my native land, English and Filipino, in addition to Pampango, the dialect of my home province. One might ask whether my bilingual faculty in Filipino and English qualifies me then as a Filipino-American writer? Observe that I hyphenated the words "Filipino" and "American," contrary to what the Chicago Manual of Style suggests. To me, one word without the other linked to it in some visual way deprives the phrase of vital meaning. I am not just Filipino, nor am I purely American. I think and feel I am both—one is inseparable from the other.

But what does this term, "Filipino-American" mean, exactly? Am I equally Filipino as I am American, or more Filipino than American? Or vice-versa? I admit I have always preferred to write in English—proof perhaps for my fellow Philippine writers that I am merely a neocolonial agent. Indeed, I struggle to write even a half-decent sentence in Filipino, these days. After twenty years in the United States, I tend to forget how to say things in my native tongue, tripping over the words and comically inventing vocabulary that sound like terms I can't momentarily recover from that part of my brain that stores the tapestry of my multi-lingual memory containing names for concepts and feelings the English language hasn't even begun to dream of! Pity, for the best I seem to be able to achieve after I employ my native tongue is a resulting harder accent on my English-speak that immediately betrays the last encounter I've had. My American husband and children are quick to note this when it happens and tease me accordingly. "You've been chatting with Filipinos again, haven't you, Mom?" I'm surprised at how this hits me with a fleeting sense of guilt, as if I've committed a crime, as if somehow, speaking my native language has taken away from my powers as an English-speaking-and-writing creature. And while I'm not sure whether I've graduated into dreaming in English, I do know that I think, speak and write better and faster in English than in any other language in my waking hours. And yet, the sentiments and ruminations in my writing? As Filipino as "Pinoy spaghetti"—the Filipinized version of an already Americanized interpretation of a European pasta dish that, if the writer who called himself Marco Polo is to be believed, was in turn inspired by Chinese noodles. Savor that! And so, *Filipino-American*? By all means! But only as a compromise, since I can't think of a better term to call myself. The less complicated evil, you see.

The seemingly convoluted path of this query and my so far inane-sounding conclusion leads my practical, skeptical self to ask, "But how is it all worth this trouble—meaning, how does the question of writer's identity even matter to one's writing?" "Write what you know," is what writing teachers always tell the beginners among us. If I only need write what I know, then why does it matter whether or not I am conscious of my identity as a writer? Should not my identity simply follow as a matter of course from the substance of my writing? Or does my awareness of my identity as a writer sub-jectively affect the objectivity of my writing? Or—and let's be frank about this—is this only really relevant to the commercial question of who my target readers are, i.e., my market? And if this market is perceived to cover only a minority of the United States reading population, does this then significantly restrict how widely I am going to get published or whether I am going to be published at all? And—who gets to decide this all-important question?

Not one to easily give in to writer's despair, I want to believe that with enough talent, discipline, and hard work, I could fairly succeed as an immigrant writer in this country—my very own American Dream! After all, there have been Filipino expatriate writers such as Eric Gamalinda, Carlos Peñaranda, Linda Casper Ty, Jessica Hagedorn, Ninotchka Rosca, and before them, Carlos Bulosan, Jose Garcia Villa, and N. V. M. Gonzales who all seemed to have succeeded in bridging the gap between language and culture to build significant following in United States literary circles. We might also reasonably assume that it must have helped the immigrant poet's cause when the 2013 Presidential Inauguration Committee chose poet Richard Blanco, a son of Cuban immigrants, to read his poem *One Today* during the inauguration program. Or did it? Could Blanco have been merely the chosen token immigrant performer for the purpose of gratifying the large Hispanic voting population that successfully carried Barack Obama into the second term of his presidency? Or was Blanco's selection truly a sign that mainstream American poetry indeed was now more willing to define itself in terms inclusive of traditions and influences that go beyond its dominant Western, Anglo-Saxon origins? Perhaps so, but not because of Blanco's poem, certainly. There appears nothing distinctly Latino or "immigrant" in Blanco's poem, apart from the persona of the poet himself. It's likely that Blanco, in his abundant generosity of spirit as many poets tend to have, purposefully wrote a poem that focused on the theme of a unified, generic America as is proper for an inauguration poem. The poem seems to avoid precisely any hint of the poet's Latino immigrant heritage thus adroitly preempting its audience from possibly dwelling upon an image of the United States as an increasingly fragmented society where the former white majority is steadily receding and feeling threatened by a burgeoning number of minorities arising from various immigrant populations, and thus, from the reality that such immigrant constituencies are now redefining our concepts of beauty, culture, values, and rights; indeed, challenging our very concept of "America" itself. And maybe this is where we're going with the question, "Who is the American writer?"

Perhaps the American writer cannot be defined simply in terms of place or location. Thus, writing or residing within the United States is largely irrelevant. Nor can it be defined, surely, by mere citizenship or nationality roots. Thus, having been born or raised in the United States, while a significant element of identity, is not an exclusive factor. Note for instance how some descendants of Muslim immigrants seem to have great difficulty in identifying with the Western societies in which they were born. Which thus raises culture, as opposed to place of birth, as defining identity. In this regard, however, what is American culture? What indeed is it, if not a kaleidoscope of many varied cultures? Perhaps being an "American" writer is simply an abstraction, an intangible concept, just as America itself is a conceptual ideal—a rogue nation formed by immigrants that dared rebel against a king and declared itself a government of the people, by the people, and for the people committed to principles of life, liberty, and the pursuit of happiness. But does this mean then that anyone in the world who believes in such principles is an "American"? The answer is, of course, no. There is as yet no nationality or citizenship by belief system. On the other hand, these arguably distinct American ideals could be said to be no less than universal human values, much like the Declaration of Human Rights. Here again, we resist the temptation to digress into an extended discussion appropriate for another essay.

So what, then, is an "American"? Perhaps "being American" is a confluence of many factors such as, but not limited to place, nationality, and conviction—the alchemy of parts instead of the mathematical sum of such parts that produces an identity that can only be fulfilled in consciousness of "being" instead of mere legal status. I surmise that similar notions inspired the Dream Act, for example. Lack of visas and passports certainly do not prevent children of insufficiently documented immigrants who were raised in this country to see themselves as "American." It is the same for the "American" writer. An immigrant poet in the United States becomes an "American" writer by the same process of "being", to the same extent that she is empowered to assimilate herself in the culture and literary traditions of this nation of many nations and witnesses her work likewise embraced and owned by the larger body of literature identified as "American." The circumstances and fate of the immigrant poet is no different, after all, from the circumstances and fate of the immigrant group from which she arose.

Which leads us back to one of our core questions, "What is American poetry?" My answer, confined to the scope of this essay, is as simple as this: American poetry is what its gatekeepers publish. And that is why it is crucial to examine the criteria by which the gatekeepers decide what or who gets to be published.

Herein thus lie the second challenge for immigrant poets—an issue that goes beyond writer's identity. I doubt it can be denied that contemporary mainstream American poetry still draws its dominant voice, substance, and style from its Anglo-Saxon roots, along with its underlying philosophical foundation that appears, in the last century, to have been keenly informed by the existentialist, post-modern movement that arose from the maturation of the capitalist-industrial state. And I bet many immigrant writers coming from different sociopolitical-economic environments that have only begun to follow the early developmental stages of the modern Western state do not share this worldview. Given this premise, the question arises therefore whether an underlying bias for a certain philosophical orientation may, in fact, be determinative of literary style and institutional patronage. If it does, then what happens to writing whose philosophical foundations do not conform to this qualifying framework?

One could observe this dynamic in the kind of poetry that continues to find favor with many ivory tower publications today. You *know* what I mean—that kind of poetry that strikes the average reader or listener as something akin to navigating a maze of riddles within a riddle that, in the end, makes one wonder whether the poet indeed wanted to connect with a real, human audience or was only enamored with the sound of his intellect verbalizing itself. It compels those of us who expect more from poetry to ask, "What was the point of it all?" not unlike perhaps the experience of the disenchanted subjects in the story of *The Emperor's New Clothes*. I suspect it is this cold, brooding, self-absorbed, or impossibly abstract poetry favored by the traditional gatekeepers that has turned off and alienated masses of otherwise would-be poetry enthusiasts who may have given up on poetry because they are fed up with the products of a literary elite that does nothing for them other than condescend upon them with presumptuous notions about their humanity or the meaning and, more accurately, the lack of it in their lives.

Which brings us to a specific philosophical issue: Should poetry merely describe the human condition, rigidly committed to pointing out nothing more than the meaninglessness and absurdity of human life? Or should poetry aspire to offer something else, something humanizing, something that threads upon the finely textured grey zones between the black and white world of art for art's sake and the world that hangs on to, borrowing the words of Blanco's patron, the "audacity of hope?"

For me, the ultimate value of poetry and other forms of creative writing lies not in the mere exposition of the existential human condition, but in facilitating man's search for meaning. In this, Victor E. Frankl's book, *Man's Search For Meaning*, shows its lasting impression on me since I'd read it in Philosophy 101. At the core of the theory of logotherapy that Frankl expounds in his book is the belief that man's primary motivational force is his search for meaning, that man could withstand anything, as long as he can somehow assign some value or significance to his life. This is especially crucial for the immigrant's experience. Around the world, people in all walks of life continue to struggle to make sense of their lives, especially those driven from their homes and native countries in search of a better life. Having lost the anchor of their homeland, and along with this, much of what is familiar and dear to them, immigrants struggle to re-create and redefine their individual and social identities in their new environments, sometimes, in the face of much persecution and discrimination. Their struggle is compounded by the immediate material necessity of establishing viable means of livelihood to provide for themselves and their families—often, to just keep body and soul together. It is in the midst of such great suffering that many immigrants might question the purpose of their struggle, until they are reminded of the soulful aspect of their exile: their desire to support their loved ones, many of whom are still back in the motherland, desperately relying on them for their most basic necessities. I find that it is in these moments— these dark nights of the soul—that the power of poetry to soothe, heal, and enlighten is most potent and thus, necessary. The literary masterpieces that stand out to me in this regard are those of writers and poets who seem to have been successful in decoding some aspect of the great mystery of life and have left their work as maps to help us navigate a meaningful path to a way of living and being that aims far beyond mere existence.

Like everything that aspires to greatness, poetry has the puissance to allow us a glimpse of the best and worst versions of ourselves. In exploring the freedoms offered by this immense power, I find a couple of principles in fiction-writing to be helpful. First, a writer must depict how the main character has evolved by the end of the story. In poetry, I, the author, am the first to be changed by the exercise of the creative process itself. But equally important to me, it is the reader or listener who, I hope, is also moved, if not changed by the experience. Yet how can I move my reader if he can barely understand what I'm saying? Thus, along with self-expression, I aspire to be understood, first and foremost. Second, I strive to write poems that suggest a glimmer of hope, no matter how faint, to sustain the reader's and perhaps, more importantly, *my* own faith in human nature. In so doing, I know I am going against the grain of mainstream American poetry, for I am allowing my work to become vulnerable to criticisms of being "sentimental" by the gatekeepers who seem to worship absolute detachment as the ideal standard of writing discipline and aesthetic, if not literary merit. Nevertheless, I refuse to be the "literary orphan" lamented by David Foster Wallace, as he describes in his novel, *Infinite Jest*:

> Postmodern irony and cynicism's become an end in itself, a measure of hip sophistication and literary savvy. Few artists dare to try to talk about ways of working toward redeeming what's wrong, because they'll look sentimental and naive to all the weary ironists. Irony's gone from liberating to enslaving ... The postmodern founders' patricidal work was great, but patricide produces orphans, and no amount of revelry can make up for the fact that writers my age have been literary orphans throughout our formative years.

Perhaps my single advantage over writers raised or educated in the United States is this: I am not the literary orphan that Wallace mourns, not only because I refuse to be one, but because I am *not* one. My literary roadmaps covered a more expansive terrain compared to the monolithic program provided by the average United States high school curriculum. For instance, we read the Rubáiyát of Omar Khayyám as early as my junior high school year in my small Philippine hometown. This was the catalyst that got me interested in other literary traditions such as those of the Persians, the Russians, the Chinese (Confucius), and the Japanese (haiku), in addition to the works of American and British masters that, along with the works of our Spanish-Filipino *maestros*, formed the foundation of our literature curriculum. It struck me thus as both comical and tragic when some of my students in the Midwest community college where I used to teach mistook the Rubáiyát as a name for a new Islamic terrorist group, and Omar Khayyam as another wanted Al-Queda leader.

As writers in the Philippines, we were encouraged to address as wide a readership as possible. This was especially emphasized in my alma mater, the University of the Philippines, where our expected audience was not restricted to the lofty halls of the academe. Indeed, my education and training in the literary arts had always urged creative endeavor in the service of effecting social change. By its very nature, this undertaking required that my work be accessible to the masses—to the "everyday" person, or what we call in the Philippines the "common *tao*"—without succumbing to what was merely pedestrian or popular. We saw our vocation as artists not in keeping the suffering masses of humanity quagmired in their misery, but rather transformed by it and thereby redeemed from it. This remains my goal as a writer in the United States.

Immediately, one sees how contradictory this perspective is from the post-modern ironists' standard of pure philosophical congruence with their art. Whereas the latter seem to seek no more than to describe what they see as reality—that is, that man's life is basically an exercise in the absurd and there is no meaning to man's existence apart from the meaning that man, through his foolish illusions and Polyannic addictions may assign to it, the literary philosophical orientation in which I was schooled questions reality and proposes on the contrary that it could be changed, not superficially as a way to escape the truth, but to shape it by the shaping of the mind. *Mind over matter.* From this, it isn't difficult to see why my desire for my poems' accessibility to the average reader does not always translate into access to publishing resources in the United States.

Which brings me back to the issue of institutional patronage, to the gatekeepers of American poetry. These literary guardians may deny it all they want, but it appears to me that contemporary mainstream American poetry is still mainly an insular art form. Its patronage continues to be dominated, if not monopolized by a small, elitist circle cultivated by the nepotistic system between Master of Fine Arts ("MFA") students, graduates, and professors, on the one hand, and their university presses and allied literary journals, on the other. Right away, one could see the acute challenges this presents to the immigrant poet, especially one who is probably reinventing herself from a career in an entirely different field that she'd pursued in her native country, who is mainly self-taught in the literary arts (meaning, she didn't spend the fifty to one hundred thousand dollars cost of tuition plus living expenses to obtain an MFA in writing or poetry), and thus, could easily be spotted as an outsider by the American literary elite.

The immigrant poet's sense of isolation and alienation is further compounded by her multicultural literary influences. For the effect of such diverse traditions on the writer, I believe, is nothing less than to affect voice and style that, I suspect, are sometimes mistaken by the gatekeepers (who may not be familiar with other writing traditions and styles or are simply not accepting of them), for lack of artistic merit and integrity. This relates to my earlier statement that the diverse literary heritage reflected in my work may be preventing me from being seen as an American poet and writer: My writing does not make me sound like one.

One could see in the stark differences between the background and perspective of the post-modern armchair philosopher-writer and the experiences of the marginalized, working-class immigrant, a clash of worldviews and traditions that are marked by corresponding differences in voice and style which an immigrant poet can only hope her colleagues inside elite American literary circles might be able to acknowledge and respect as "different but equal." While it is all right, for instance, for the armchair philosopher-writer to describe Tiananmen Square with—

> Steady whir of metal wheels,
> punctuated by cobbled gaps,
> press on steadfast path, leaving
> red coats in their dust…
> (my composition, to demonstrate my point)),

I suspect that the working class immigrant, particularly the refugee who'd had to escape death by the thread of his meager shirt, will more readily understand and empathize with what happened in Tiananmen Square through verse clothed with the voice and style exemplified by Neruda in the following last stanza of his poem, "I Explain Some Things":

> Come and see the blood in the streets,
> come and see

the blood in the streets,
come and see the blood
in the streets!

The difference in voice and style of above poems can be likened to how one might prefer cool jazz and how another likes hot salsa music instead. It's no less yet no more than a difference in cultural and philosophical temperament! Even my use of exclamation points here to accentuate my tone can be frowned upon as unnecessary and symptomatic of amateur writing by stiff-upper-lipped gatekeepers who invented a rule against using exclamation points for professional expository writing that, to me, operates to coerce me into settling for the blandness of a period—and thus, adopting the personality of their writing style as my own! Tell me, honestly, if the average editor of a literary journal in America today were to receive a poem that contained Neruda's lines such as above poem without knowing the poem was Neruda's, would such editor be predisposed to publish it? What is the likelihood of a poem getting published that has similar direct, raw, naked, tender, passionate, and confrontational qualities as Neruda's poems, whose meaning is not hidden behind some high-minded riddle one has to solve before its message hits the heart—in other words, a poem that will probably be judged as "sentimental" by the gatekeepers of American poetry? Whitman knew the answer to this question long before Neruda came along. Is it any wonder then that the American master had to resort, initially, to publishing his own poems? His poetic style and voice were radically different from what was considered mainstream American poetry in his day as to have amounted to a revolutionary form, so that Whitman surely knew that the only way he could reach his audience while he was still alive was by directly reaching out to them.

We see a resurgence in this strategy today among immigrant poets and writers who are no longer waiting for nor relying upon validation from the traditional gatekeepers to manifest their acceptance into the world not only of American but also global literature. The previously marginalized poet is empowered by the democratizing, liberating, and globalizing effect of the Internet. Digital technology and social media are revolutionizing how the poet publishes his work and how the reader accesses and shares it. In the marketplace of ideas, the best, or at least, the most enduring ideas sell; the most inspiring, honest, relevant poetry is read and passed on to friends of friends of friends; and technology has become the new gatekeeper that is fast replacing the old guards, so that the criterion of who gets to enter the gates of the literary world becomes mainly the transcendent merit or mass appeal of a writer's work, not the tyrannical censorship of the old autocracy.

Contemporary publishing entrepreneurs have been quick to recognize this revolution, seizing upon the vast economic opportunities it presents to both themselves and writers. By offering increasingly sophisticated self-publishing platforms that not only allow writers greater access to publication and marketing resources but fairer royalty payment structures, they meld writers' goals with corporate profitability. Indeed more and more experienced writers are rejecting the traditional publishing route in favor of self-publishing because of the exploitative royalty contracts offered by most traditional publishers. And ironically, more and more traditional publishers are looking into track records in what otherwise the more conservative among them eschew as vanity publishing to decide whether to take a chance on the work of upcoming writers. The new breed of publishing professionals are socially-savvy gatekeepers that continue to ensure that the gates don't merely become loose floodgates of arbitrary, vain self-promotion. They do this by offering various editing and related services that help their writers observe essential literary standards. In so doing, they show that they recognize they are only keeping up with what their market readership demands in a vast sea of writing flotsam and jetsam through literary products that not only entertain but also possess authentic, enduring artistic merit. In the end, the final judge of who gets inside the gates is the validating power of the patronage of a mass yet discriminating audience that is reclaiming its freedom of choice from what otherwise are merely publishing middlemen who have usurped and quite possibly abused the role of literary police. One wonders whether the traditional gatekeepers are the dinosaurs of our time, or whether they will evolve to adapt to this brave new world of publishing if, for nothing else, than to save themselves from obsolescence and extinction. Little did they know that Whitman might have been prophesying not only about the American socio-cultural-political landscape but also to its literary institutions when he wrote in "Crossing Brooklyn Ferry," "others will enter the gates."

Of course the irony of all of this is that with the globalization of literary publishing and distribution through the Internet and other forms and platforms of technology comes what I believe will be the inevitable internationalization of literary subject, form, style, and voice that, in effect, will make all our current musings and debates on what is and what is not American poetry and writing, or who is and who is not the American poet and writer quite simply moot and academic. Every writer evolves at some point, if one were to be a writer of true substance and note, into a citizen of the world and child of humanity. I believe that all great writing aspires to achieve an essential universal quality that I think the immigrant poet and writer—who traverses multiple worlds, transcends their boundaries, and successfully transcribes the individual human condition into the annals of humanity's common heritage and legacy—is especially privileged to envision, and thus, achieve.

Whitman's poetry, just like Neruda's, stands the test of time precisely because the thoughts, emotions, and ideas contained therein are as timeless and universal as human nature itself. People hate or love; fall to ruin or overcome adversity; die or survive; fade away or spawn new generations. *The circle of life.* This, we understand. This, we only need to re-hear in fresh ways—in ways that speak to our minds and hearts in beauty and grace or in ugliness so gross that, by itself, is beautiful. In ways that do not patronize us nor condescend upon us. These, immigrant poets and writers can deliver, and technology has empowered us to do so by enabling us to crash the gates of the old guards.

We have already entered the gates, and there is no turning back.

Notes

1. Grageda-Smith, Maria Victoria A., *Warrior Heart, Pilgrim Soul: An Immigrant's Journey, Pilgrim Books, 2013, p. 88.*

Poetry Brings Out the Mexican in Me
Rigoberto González

I.

I identify as Chicano, a term that situates me, politically and geo-graphically, within the borders of the United States. It's a term I've learned to embrace since my days in college when I declared myself part of a community, a social movement, a legacy. The word gave me orientation when I needed it the most, when I realized I had moved out of my Mexican family's home permanently. Chicano offered me a direction: it was forward-thinking, it was progressive, and yet it often reached back to my Mexican roots because it valued memory, history, and story.

As I moved on the professional path as a writer, the more deliber-ate and vocal I became about declaring my identity as a Chicano. I was a Chicano writer. Though by this time I had also come out of the closet, so now I was a gay Chicano writer or a queer Latino writer, depending on context. To me these are more than labels or catego-ries; they are commitments and responsibilities to my communi-ties, and an acknowledgement of my journey so far. These choices don't measure my distance away from my youth when I identified as a Mexican, they highlight my growing circle of associations, my ever-expanding family.

I resist calling myself an American writer because to me it erases those exchanges and interactions that shaped me as a politicized citizen and an artist. It's true, I'm an American writer, but more true is my loyalty to and recognition of my ethnicity and sexual orientation. I celebrate them by keeping them close to my name: *Rigoberto González, gay Chicano writer.* If I uphold them as badges of honor, it's because these identities—like all minority identities—tend to be devalued. To me, they are declarations of pride.

Additionally, I've always found the adjective "American" problematic. American is of the Americas, a landmass that stretches from Canada's Boothia Peninsula to Chilean Patagonia's Cape Forward. But a patriotic fervor has co-opted the word to signify strictly a U.S. identity. And American patriotism has always come across to me as limned with xenophobic sentiment, which pushes against my other important identity: immigrant.

II.

In a nutshell: I was born in Bakersfield, California in 1970; my family returned to its homeland Michoacán in 1972; we moved back to the U.S. in 1980; and my family returned to Mexico again, leaving me behind because I was enrolled in college, in 1992. I was only a resident of Michoacán for a very brief period, but it was an important one in terms of shaping my consciousness about who I was in relation to the world: I was Mexican, I spoke Spanish, but I grew up learning about the North from the dubbed television programs and in the evenings I heard entertaining stories about California from my father and Abuela, who had lived many years there. As a child I longed to have my own stories about the North, and eventually it would happen since all the moving back and forth from one country to another was the González way to survive. Our move North in 1980 wasn't entirely unexpected, though that didn't make it any easier to adjust.

Growing up in Southern California, in a farmworking community, meant that all things Mexican and all things Spanish were at home. All things American, all things English were at school. This demarcation would have been troubling if it didn't afford me a private world: at home, my American space was my homework and the many books I read; at school, my Mexican space was in my imagination—what else did I have to think or write about if it wasn't stories about my family and Mexico? It was ironic to find myself longing for both when I had long anticipated, long looked forward to, life in the North.

I suppose this bicultural bilingual identity prepared me for my future as a Chicano, where such complexities in an upbringing were not unusual and much appreciated as strengths in a person's character. I realized this very quickly in social settings, when suddenly my peers would start comparing Abuela anecdotes and giggling at the similarities among our oddball Mexican fathers, our dysfunctional Mexican homes. It appears that in college I was also nurturing the material that would eventually find its way into my writing, poetry in particular. Whenever I started to think about writing a poem, the process brought out the Mexican in me.

III.

I'm frequently asked if my poems, written exclusively in English, are translated into Spanish. This question makes me bristle because it seems to imply that my work isn't good enough in the language it's already written in. In the past, I would simply say no, but apologetically, as if I had done something wrong. But now I simply state the truth: what for? My audience is an English-speaking, English-reading audience. And although I'm fluent in Spanish, I'm not reaching out to Spanish-speakers. Or maybe I am since I'm certain that part of my English-speaking, English-reading audience is also bilingual or multilingual or culturally versed in the Mexican/ Chicano/ Latino landscape I inhabit. In any case, English isn't my imposed limitation. It's my chosen tool to communicate, mostly because my literary education has been in English.

The other question that irks me is when I'm asked if I code-switch or employ intralingual devices in my work. Again, no, and I probably never will. As I explained earlier, my family was very clear about keeping a border between the two languages. My grandfather especially would become furious if we peppered Spanish with English words. He considered it a corruption of the language, at best, at worst, a lack of education. My brother and I, of course, would code-switch in the privacy of our room, as a kind of defiance to Abuelo's prejudices, but we knew this was a forced speech. It didn't come naturally to us at all the way we heard it spoken in our neighborhoods, by our closest friends.

In college I encountered the work of Alurista, Juan Felipe Herrera, Sandra Cisneros, and other poets who did code-switch, and I understood the work perfectly, but could not imitate it without feeling like an impostor. It seemed I was, like Abuelo, very Mexican in my thinking that this was the language of the pochos, the American born and raised Mexicans. Like them, I too was Chicano. But unlike me, they were not Mexican.

IV.

I call *So Often the Pitcher Goes to Water until It Breaks* (1999), my first book, my love letter to Mexico. I began writing this book as my graduate school thesis in 1992, the year my entire family relocated to

Michoacán once again, leaving me in its adopted country all alone. I remember Abuela calling me on the phone to ask if I was going to pack my bags as well, and we both knew that I would stay, that I had another path to follow. That goodbye made me want to hold on to what appeared to be slipping through my fingers like sand. I remember that as soon as I hung up the phone I started writing things down, as if I was afraid of forgetting. I had done this once before when I was ten, on our three-day bus ride from Michoacán to the U.S.-Mexico border: I stared wide-eyed out the window, taking it all in because I was losing it all, my country, my home, one small town at a time.

Over the years, when I make appearances at college campuses, I have come to expect the question about this separation from family. A young man or woman, clearly homesick, identifying with me as the child of immigrants, comes up to me to inquire how I did it: How did I not simply pack my bags and go back home?

Home? Home is the word and the work. As an artist, I understand that home is an imagined space and that I'm always imagining, therefore I'm never not home. But this is such an abstract and philosophical concept, and it took me years to believe it myself. Because, yes, there were long periods of loneliness and emptiness, short periods of second-guessing and regrets. So instead, I offer them my "string theory." It's an immigrant's way of reconciling with the legacy of migration.

I tell the anxious young person: "You need a piece of string and a map of the Americas. Now hold one end of the string on the place of the map that marks the beginning of your parents's journey, where they come from. Now stretch the string to the place on the map where they set up a home or to where you were born. That's the length of your parents's journey, your parents who likely didn't have the same opportunities and education that you have had so far. Now, how much are you going to add to that string if you don't even dare leave home?"

The demonstration works every time because these young people acquired a fear that their own parents didn't have. Or rather, they forgot about a strength and courage that is their immigrant legacy.

If my parents stretched that string from Michoacán to California, I have stretched it from California to New York City. There were many temporary homes along the way in Arizona, New Mexico, Ohio and Illinois—my peripatetic nature mirrored my family's, always moving on to the next job. But no matter where I was, when I sat down to write I inhabited the memory of Mexico. I recall at one point, finishing my childhood memoir *Butterfly Boy: Memories of a Chicano Mariposa*, in Scotland. That's the immigrant's complexity: you leave home, yet you never leave home, or rather, the body leaves home, but home never leaves the body. There is a beautiful comfort in that, which doesn't allow loneliness to settle in.

V.

As a man in my forties, three decades removed from the homeland of my childhood, I'm feeling an insatiable nostalgia for home. That doesn't mean I want to return to Mexico (I've been lucky enough to visit about every other year), but I do want to return to what reminds me of home—Spanish. It's my first language, my first introduction to song, poetry, storytelling, and every other artistic discipline. And so I play the music of my elders, what I grew up listening on the record player—Las Jilguerillas, Lola Beltrán, and Abuela's *pirekuas* sung in her native Tarasco tongue, Purépecha. I read Neruda, García Lorca, and Vallejo in Spanish. I hold long conversations with my Spanish-speaking friends and family over the phone. No, I have not lost my language, but I have to make a concerted effort to engage with it.

I don't quite understand this desire but I remember seeing it in my father and his brother when they were my age. They longed for what they had left behind in their youth as well and so they dug out all the archived posters and other memorabilia of their band, *Dinastía*, and displayed them prominently on the walls. The dates, 1973, 1974, so long ago, so far away in the small stages of Michoacán. Perhaps this renewed appreciation is simply the body coming to terms with growing old. But I like to think of it as valuing what has not been forgotten, despite the distance of time and place.

I don't have the kinds of relics my father and uncle saved. Since I separated from my parents and my homeland at such a young age, whatever I've kept has been preserved only through memory and in my writing. Maybe that's why Spanish has become more important now than it was in my 20s and 30s. I want to hear those memories, those words, in their native tongue. Maybe that's why poetry, in particular, demands to be Mexican in its inspiration.

VI.

My most recent book of poetry, *Unpeopled Eden* (2013), is dedicated to my father, and to my 4-year-old nephew. My father died in Mexico, my nephew was born there, and still lives there. The poems speak to the immigrant's journey, sometimes painful and devastating. It also speaks to the loss of fathers who migrate without their families, who abandon their families, who die far from their families and homelands. When I wrote the book, the shadow of my own father's death loomed over me, as if I was working my way through the loss. Looking at my father's decisions, his life journey, through the lens of conditions shaped by socio-economic necessities, by political climates, allowed me to steer clear of personal accusations, of reducing my perception of him as a series of disappointments and heartbreaks. I included my nephew in the vision of the book as a way of inserting a glimmer of hope. There are some of us whose father comes back, the way my brother did, to his children.

The more I read from that book, the more I've come to understand my own place in it, maybe in the world I live in. In many ways, I am like those fathers. I left Mexico and never went back. Is it not socio-economic necessity that compelled me to stay behind in this country where I saw a future for myself as an educated man? Is not political climate that informed my choice to gravitate toward spaces that welcomed my ethnicity, embraced my sexuality? As much as I claim *Unpeopled Eden* is about the immigrant, or my father, or those men who disappear, who perish, who dissolve into the horizon, it is perhaps the most autobiographical of my poetry books.

As I watch daylight fade into darkness, I am safe and comfortable in my little studio in Queens, NY. I don't have to go anywhere if I don't want to. But my mind does. It wanders and explores in ways my immigrant body can't or doesn't need to anymore. I've traveled to many places on the planet, but still I return to my beloved Mexican landscape, and to the stories that remind me that this is who we Mexicans—we migrant souls—are, curious about the next place, sentimental about the last one.

Home, Again
An Immigrant Writer's Meditation on the Meaning of Home
Kwame Dawes

I have lived in the United States for twenty-four years—just about half my life. Like most immigrants, a declaration of that nature is startling because of how ordinary it is. For many of us, there is a point at which we realize that we have lived in the United States or in some other country where we are aliens for longer than we lived in our "home country." And no matter what we choose to call that home country to assuage this sense of absurdity (mother country, homeland, yard, home, etc.) we are nonetheless having to come to terms with the idea that one's idea of belonging is rarely defined by chronology, but by the peculiarity of first knowledge, first definitions of self.

The problem, though, in my case, is that at gut level, when I say I am going home, I am often referring to Jamaica. This country is not my mother's country (although it is where she lives now), not my country of birth, not my country of citizenship nor even where I have spent most of my life. I was born in Ghana, and when I was ten years old or so, we moved to Jamaica. I lived in Jamaica for the next seventeen years before moving to Canada to study. Admittedly, while I was in Canada, I was a Jamaican resident and in every sense I never regarded my six years in Canada as that of an immigrant. I was a student and I was planning to return to Jamaica after those five years getting my Ph.D. and the next year and half working there while I sought a job. Indeed, I was certain that I would be returning to Jamaica to do a job that I was perfectly suited for—a kind of natural fit. I had been assured that on my return I would assume a position as drama tutor at the Creative Arts Centre, a place where I had spent most of my undergraduate and graduate years at the University of the West Indies, developing my craft as a playwright and director.

The thing is that anyone meeting me in those days assumed me to be a Jamaican, and I saw no reason to suggest otherwise. Of course, while I was in Canada, I did not abandon my Ghanaian status. I still carried a Ghanaian passport and I was a Ghanaian citizen. And I never denied being Ghanaian, indeed it was an important part of how I introduced myself. In that sense, I was behaving about Ghana in a manner no different from what I did when I lived in Jamaica. When I lived in Jamaica, I knew I was Jamaican, but I also knew I was a different kind of Jamaican. I was an immigrant to Jamaica.

I had never secured Jamaican citizenship, and I never, not until I was in my late twenties, thought that my Jamaicaness would ever be in question. I was comfortably Jamaican and Ghanaian. In Canada, I was vice president of the African Student Union and vice president of the Caribbean Circle at the same time. The Africans were sometimes a little skeptical about my bonafides because I did not speak any other Ghanaian language but English. I spoke Spanish and some French which made me even more squarely Caribbean. I was studying Caribbean literature and I was the lead singer of two reggae bands. I played cricket with a team in Fredericton. Finally I spoke the Jamaican language with ease and confidence. And when I was away from Canada, when I went home, I was going to Jamaica. That was where my mother was, that was where all my siblings lived.

Still, I remained unable to, and quite unwilling to deny or push back my Ghanaian status. I had so many relatives in Ghana, and I had strong and defining memories of Ghana that I could not and would not push aside. I was also studying African literature with gusto and authority. It was not complicated for me to be both African and Caribbean, and at the end of the day, whatever I defined as my home place was somewhat irrelevant to the fact that I was an alien in the country where I was studying.

By the time I moved to the United States, I had refined this narrative of home with a set answer. People in South Carolina would say, "You are not from here," and I would say, "Right." "The islands?" they would ask. "Kind of." And then if I felt like it I would offer the quick and dirty narrative: "I was born in Ghana, West Africa, and moved to Jamaica when I was a child. I grew up in Jamaica. It is Jamaica that you are hearing." Most people latched onto the Jamaican thing, feeling proud that they could discern a Jamaican accent. "I was in Jamaica once, really nice. Great beaches." I would smile. And on some occasions, it would be Ghana that would engage them. It was one of several things: the Peace Corp, a church missionary trip, a good friend who was married to a Ghanaian or some version of Ghanaian, which would be African. What I wasn't, was American, and certainly not African American.

I am not sure when exactly I became African American, but I can say that it was a political decision and not an emotional one. On census forms I tick African American. I have joined the force. I would say that it happened in the mid-nineties, a few years into my time in the US. In my head I understood that my narrative, my history was different, but I also knew that there was something disquieting about the ways in which (and here I generalize, though not inaccurately) white people sought to emphasize (usually as a compliment to me) my non-African Americanness and my alien status, and the way that African Americans suspected my blackness and certainly any hint of my African American status. This would change, I think, when I came to the realization that my greatest challenge about being African American, was not the "African" part of the equation, but the "American" part of the equation. I wrote a whole book about it. The book was called, *A Far Cry from Plymouth Rock*. It is an immigrant's personal narrative, and in many ways it is a meditation on my relationship with America. But it is, also, a meditation on my relationship with Jamaica, a country upon which I had foisted my Jamaican identity—I demanded it, I continue to demand it, and I have done so even when I do not have a fully realized legal claim to it.

Technically, I *am* Jamaican—by law, with my father being Jamaican, and my grandparents on my father's side being Jamaican, I have, by Jamaican law, absolute right to Jamaican citizenship. But this right is complicated by the fact that my father was not born in Jamaica. He was, in fact, born in Africa, in Warri, Nigeria. He was still under five (perhaps two years old) when he moved to Jamaica but he became a Jamaican citizen by naturalization. Had this not been the case, his birth certificate would have sufficed to secure me and my siblings automatic citizenship. Had I been living continuously in Jamaica during the period when I started to do the work of securing Jamaican citizenship, again the process would have been simple enough as it has been for my siblings. But as it stands now, I am working on the paper work to secure citizenship, a process that has taken a few years because it involved much research to prove my grandparent's status, their parentage of my father, and then his parentage of me. Seems simple enough, right? Not with the ages we are dealing with. In the process, though, I have been able to trace my Jamaican family as far back as the late eighteen-century, which is not bad given the way these things could go. I am hoping to have a legal right to call myself Jamaican by the end of the year.

It was far easier to become an American. And the above paragraph may lead to a call from the US government because, as I understand it, America has secured exclusive rights to my citizenship. I don't find this complicated. I would have a clear answer to the query. I am simply attempting to legitimize a historical fact—that I am Jamaican and that Jamaica, if it so desires, can claim me in some way. And Jamaica has. I am a Jamaican writer. This is what Jamaica says about me. After all, I am somewhat skeptical that America, as a nation, will feel an emotional affinity to me. And yet, parts of America have expressed such a connection. South Carolina's granting me one of the highest honors it can grant an artist was not casually done. I felt an affinity and I welcomed that recognition. It was a mature act by the state because it was expanding its notion of citizenry to include recent immigrants like myself. This meant a great deal to me.

There are, of course, significant implications to me as a professional writer, when it comes to this matter of my national identity. Becoming an American citizen certainly has made travel as a writer easier and less hampered by long delays in customs and immigration—especially in Miami: not sure what that is about. It has also allowed me to qualify for a number of literary awards that are open to only US citizens. Beyond that, I have to say that Americans tend not to be as interested in one's legal status when it comes to recognizing a writer's right to write about America. The green card remains the ticket. With that in hand, Americans like immigrant writers to acknowledge their immigrant status even as they speak as Americans. It is the one concession demanded. Few people, especially immigrants, quarrel with this, largely because at some level, they want that kind of deniability—the ability to say, I am an American, but my Americanness is different, it is complicated by my coming from somewhere else. But my ambiguous Jamaican status has had some significant impact on my writing career. A few years ago, I was informed that I had won the regional prize for the Commonwealth Fiction prize and was one of four writers up for the overall Commonwealth Fiction Prize. The book was *A Place to Hide*, a collection of short stories that were all set in Jamaica. I had won for the Caribbean/Americas region. I am not sure exactly what the sequence of events were after that, but I do know that I initiated the inquiry and eventually I chose to, despite advice not to do so by people I trusted and respected, inform the Commonwealth Prize folks that I did not have Jamaican citizenship despite being Jamaican. They quickly withdrew the book. A person close enough to the final decision for the overall prize had told me that my book was the "front runner." I like to believe that. My publishers, Peepal Tree, had never had a conversation about citizenship with me and so, quite understandably, assumed that I had legal Jamaican citizenship. So they entered the book in that category and not in the African region as might have been wiser. Of course, its chances of succeeding in that region would have been quite limited since there was precious little that could be called African about the book. It was disappointing, and also felt a little absurd.

Since then there have been similar situations. To this day, for instance, I have not been able to contend for the Bocas Prize—a

Caribbean award for literature. Despite the fact that I am comfortably listed on any credible gathering of Caribbean writers today, including all the most recent anthologies and bibliographies, and despite the fact that my work remains deeply inscribed in the Caribbean, the fact of my citizenship as defined in the terms set out by Bocas has prevented me from being considered. Interestingly, the rules surrounding eligibility around citizenship and identity vary from place to place. Most Africa-wide awards tend to have less stringent rules on such matters. More often than not, eligibility is determined by the following criteria: born in the country, a citizen or legal resident of the country, or the child of a parent who is a native of an African country.

I have come to the realization, however, that a significant part of my motivation to write and the subject of what I write about has little to do with what I regard as my legal status to a country or a society. I realize that I am writing out of respect for, admiration for, and pleasure in a body of work that, as a reader, has helped to define who I am and how I deal in this world. That this has been inextricably connected to my complex biography of migration, my ancestry, and the circumstances of my political and cultural standing in the world only makes sense as far as I am concerned.

I believe that there are at least two critical traits for a writer that can generate energy, innovation and creativity. The first is one of belonging—a sense that one belongs to a tradition or that one wants to belong to that tradition. The tradition has to be manageable. It is one thing to think of oneself as belonging to the tradition of Shakespeare and Aristophanes and another to think of oneself as belonging to a long tradition of Nebraskan playwrights. Both claims may be true, but one is far more manageable than the other, one is far more pragmatic than the other. After all, I doubt that Shakespeare's ambition was to become the great Caribbean playwright or the great American playwright for that matter. It is evident that Shakespeare was fired up by being a part of an exciting community of writers and actors in Elizabethan London, and it was enough to make him work hard, compete, and challenge himself in ways that I think aided his greatness. It is a truism to say this but it bears repeating: Shakespeare was first profoundly parochial before we could even think of him as "universal."

I have always had the view that I write with the luggage of my history on my back and with a responsibility to contend with and embrace that history, as complicated as it is. The post-structural scholars arrived at a convenient way of describing this baggage— they called it "discourse." It is a neat way to turn slippery things like biography, emotional affinity, nationality, identity, and so on, into some "textual", something, negotiable and inevitable. I honestly do not need such neatness. I live under the useful delusion that I come from somewhere, I create, I imagine, I feel, I think all in ways that allow me to use the "I" comfortably. That said, my writing life is defined by an attempt to write into and out of the world that has shaped me and has helped me to find a language for who I am. Which is why I am happily a writer who feels in some ways that I am part of the tradition of modern African literature, as well as a part of modern Caribbean literature. I also feel comfortably positioned in the area of modern Black literature in America, and more gener-ally, though quite precisely, a part of the literature of the African Diaspora. I don't feel constrained by these labels. In fact I feel chal-lenged by them and I also feel as if I am enlarged by them. Tellingly, having lived in South Carolina for nineteen years, I was extremely comfortable and proud of being a part of the literary tradition of South Carolina. Being an immigrant in that context has never bothered me. I have always felt as if the fact that I am an immigrant in the country means that that country's literary tradition has to now expand to include the "immigrant" voice—in other words the political fact of my presence as a resident and citizen in that society means that the society has to now contend with its expanding understanding of itself. And this, I suspect, is how I understand myself to be an African American writer or a writer writing in the African American tradition. I recognize that this is a bold enough statement to make, and in many ways, I do not believe it is my claim to make. The truth is that I have embraced the labels given to me only when the people giving me the labels are the ones who have most at stake with those labels. My position as an African American can only exist as part of a larger idea of the Black American who belongs to the wider African Diaspora. And it is with this idea, this pan-African ideal, that I understand my place in the African American tradition. My confidence in this lies in the fact that my engagement with the African American tradition is visceral and defining. It has always been that way. Its distinctions are clear to me, but I understand that I have no place in that tradition unless those who have the most at stake in that tradition recognize me as belonging to it in some way. I suspect that Claude McKay had the same challenge, as did Marcus Garvey, Kwame Ture, and contemporaries like Claudia Rankine among so many others.

Make no mistake about it, the relationship between the black immigrant and the African American community has never been a straight forward one free of significant problems. One only has to consider the peculiar politics of understanding Barack Obama as an African American to really appreciate the extent of the problem. Obama, during the run up to his triumphant march to the White House, and since then, has been seen as not quite African American because no one in his family who was black, had experienced any of the signature moments of African American experience—slavery and the intense period of Jim Crow oppression. In many ways, there is a compelling way in which this fact can define the way a person views herself or how a person is received. However, there are ways in which Obama can be nothing but an African American for the narrative of his blackness is defined as much by the ways in which his direct ancestry may have lived in this country, as well as by the way in which he is a beneficiary, for better or for worse, by dint of his color, of the good and bad of being black in America. The history of slavery has had an incalculable impact on the social, political, economical and cultural experience of black people in America whether their ancestry travels as far back as the period of slavery or not. That said, the extent to which that becomes a defining factor in determining who is an African American writer, for instance, probably has everything to do with the way such a writer is received and the way that writer understands herself in this society.

Slavery is not alien to my ancestry. Is this important? I suspect so. I suspect that one of the reasons that I have found a place in South Carolina is that I found the lines that normally separate the Caribbean from the United States are somehow strained, and sometimes broken by the history of colonial South Carolina and the inextricable connection that it had with the Caribbean. When I looked at Tom Feelings' brilliant book of paintings, *The Middle Passage: White Ships/ Black Cargo*, it was clear to me that he was speaking to my ancestry as much as he was to the ancestry of African Americans. Feelings found it more important to locate the trauma of that part of history as a trauma experienced by Africa and its Diaspora. This broader understanding of identity was important to Feelings and has always given me a sense of place and self. I say always because this has been the nature of the way I was raised, the home I was raised in and the world of Jamaica in the 1970s where the struggle to affirm an affinity with Africa was neither a casual one nor one that was inevitable. I say this because I have always rested my sense of self as being a part of Africa and her diaspora—it has offered me my own manageable and expansive parochialism, one in which I could always find a rich vein of tradition and one to which I believe I can contribute. It is this quality in roots reggae music that has played a great role in me defining myself as a reggae poet. I was never, in so doing, denying my African identity or my place in Black America, but in fact, affirming it.

At the end of the day however, the question of my status as immigrant or otherwise will be immaterial. I have never sat before an empty page with the desire to affirm my nationhood or identity through the writing. I have simply sought to write as honestly and as beautifully as I can. But I am no fool. I know that this "pure" impulse is not at all "pure" or free of all the complexities of identity and place that have come to shape the writer I am and the work I write. It does, but I try to treat it as simply a given, something I won't negotiate and something that is as mysterious to me as how I determine what I will write about and how I will write about it. I don't want to know too much about the insides of these impulses. I prefer to see what comes of them when I am done with the work.

Ultimately, my work is there. It exists as a peculiar source of information about who I am as a writer and as a human being living in a world defined by the geopolitics of race and identity. A study of this aspect of my work should be quite revealing. It will become clear that I do feel at once inside and outside of all the cultures that I embrace as, in some way, my own. Above all, what I feel is profound gratitude for the permission that my entry into these worlds has given me as a writer. Every one of my books reflects, I am sure, this gratitude.

Some time ago, while preparing a piece on the meaning of place in my work, I asked myself the question: where is home? It remains unclear to me whether the rejoinder that I arrived at came from me or came from something I had read or overheard somewhere, but it continues to make sense to me. I concluded that home is where I want to be buried. But I also knew that this idea of burial was not to be understood in the way of Christian faith in which the body is merely flesh that is rotting when we die, in which the soul departs and arrives in the presence of Jesus. I do believe this. But there is another narrative of death and burial that makes sense to me and it is predicated on the idea of the ancestors, the host of welcoming witness who are inextricably tied to the temporal world. In this mythos, death arrives with the beginning of a new journey, one in which you encounter those who have passed, whole villages, whole cities, whole communities of an ancestral multitude each of whom has a vested interest in you as the person. All cultures have some form of this phenomenon built into the collective psyche of the people. It is comforting. In some cultures it is the surety of the spirit world that secures the land as where we belong somehow, as the connection that we have to place. In some cultures it is this idea of a waiting ancestry, persistent and engaged in the details of the world in which we live, that offers comfort and a sense of continuity into the future. For others it is this hope of a new encounter of welcome that ensures that even when our lives have been spent as aliens in a world that has been unwelcoming, or that has, for reasons of circumstance, left us orphans and with knowledge of where we come from, we will, upon our death, find our way to a kind of home. It is a beautiful gift that our imagination provides us with, and it is in this sense that I started to think about the idea of home. I concluded that home is as basic as the ideas of home for so many cultures around the world. Home is where the bones of the ancestors are buried not because there is inherent value in the bones, but because there is a sense that the spirits of the ancestors will remain close to where the bones are, and to be buried with those bones is to be assured that on the other side, someone, some people, a crowd of people, will be waiting there to welcome me, recognize me, connect me to a longer history of belonging, one that I think we hunger for in our temporal existence. In this iteration of home, home for me would be Jamaica or Ghana. And there is some comfort there. But I cannot say that there is not another bloodline of the imagination, of empathy and connection, of memory and adoption that is not equally compelling. This bloodline is probably what allows me as a writer to feel free to consider this place where I am now, this country full of the spirits of so many whose language I don't know, as a kind of home. Being an alien at home is hard work. It demands vigilance. It resists the desire to relax, to believe, somehow, in a love that is unconditional. And perhaps, I want to be able to relax one day.

What Is Russian About American Poetry

(If You Happen to Be a Russian-born American Poet)

Michael Dumanis

On the morning of June 9th, 1981, at the age of five years and almost five months, I left, for the only time, the Union of Soviet Socialist Republics, a place I will never return to, because it no longer exists. I never said good-bye to the country of my birth, nor did I ever say good-bye to the assembled throng of emotional relatives and family acquaintances, because no one had told me that I was permanently, irrevocably leaving. Nor did anybody tell me where we were headed, first for three days to a Red Cross shelter in Austria, then for a month to Rome, then finally to Boston. I thought we were just going on vacation to an outlying Soviet Socialist Republic, Azerbaijan, Ukraine, Uzbekistan, as we did for a month every summer the first five years of my life. But when I'd ask, my parents got uncharacteristically evasive: they thought I'd spill the beans to the wrong person or have some kind of cognitive breakdown if they told me, so instead they spun a web of elaborate, contradictory fictions about where we were headed on vacation each time I asked why we were packing and preparing for a trip.

The Aeroflot jet that once-and-for-all transported me out of the Soviet Union was headed for Kinshasa, Zaire, via Vienna, where we would deplane. I was so thoroughly confused by the sight of all the Africans at the gate that I thought, "Africa! My parents are taking me to Africa on vacation! It's a surprise! That's why they haven't told me." I remember being excited, and then disillusioned, and then apprehensive, as the days wore on, that I would never go back, that something enormous and vital was being kept from me. In truth, my mother had no idea how to tell a five-year-old that he may never see his grandmother or aunt again, that he would effectively start his life over in a new country speaking a new language. Finally, she sat me down on her bed in a fleabag *pensione* for refugees in Rome and said, "I wrote a poem, Misha. Would you like to hear it?"

This is the translated text of my mother's poem, in its entirety:

Song About How We Will Arrive in America
and What Will Happen

America is a humongous country.
It is full of everything.
It contains multitudes.
It contains many houses,
And a lot of food, enough for everyone.
Australians love snow,
And Canadians love snow,
And America is full of everything,
Even snow, enough for everyone.
If you require a kangaroo, there is no reason
To move to Australia.
Call America. You will find it in America.
It is full of everything, even kangaroos, enough for everyone.

And if you require a camel, you will find it.
America has everything, even camels.
Africa may have oppressive heat,
But in America you will also find plenty of heat,
Because it is full of everything, even heat, enough for everyone.
If you don't know the English language, it's no tragedy.
You will find it in America, because America has everything,
Even the English language, there is enough of it for everyone.
And if you happen to like songs, you will find them in
    America,
For there are plenty of songs in America, enough for everyone.

Was this the first poem, aside from children's verse, that I had ever heard? How fitting that the first poem I remember was literally news that has stayed news, a grandiose, seductive promise that I would end up in a dreamland without limits where I would discover the possibilities of the English language and plenty of songs. The poem also seemed a way, however fanciful, for my mother to reexamine her decision to immigrate to the United States, and to confront her anxiety about moving to a country where she would not be able to communicate in her first language ("if you don't know the English language, it's no tragedy"): it strikes me now that it's no accident that the other potential destinations the poem discusses are Australia, Canada, and Africa: at the time, with the exception of Israel, the only countries that readily and commonly accepted Jewish refugees from the former Soviet Union were Australia, Canada, South Africa, and the United States.

When my first collection of poems, *My Soviet Union*, was published in 2007, the first review actually came out in Russia, in *The Moscow Times*, where an American critic who clearly expected a more overt and topical focus on Soviet history or Russian-American immigrant experience from the work of an immigrant poet, argues that my collection is one where "we encounter another order of the assimilated author: the heritage speaker or early transplant whose Mother Russia is further back in the mind, a personal myth or memory, as nonexistent a country as one's own Soviet Union can be. Though he speaks Russian, Dumanis seems wholly rooted in American language and tradition."

On the one hand, the reviewer has a point: my Soviet Union is very much in my mind, a fusion of my childhood memory with my parents' ghost-and-war stories, filtered through my overactive imagination. In fact, I only returned to a literal Moscow for the first time in 2011, the thirtieth anniversary of my departure. On the other hand, I know that every poem I have written carries within it—in terms of both its thematic preoccupations and its technical and rhetorical choices—a Soviet-born and immigrant-stamped DNA. There is nothing illusory about my bilingualism, which refracts my every English utterance into a Russian utterance inside my head and offers me two divergent and contradictory syntactic possibilities anytime I try to string some words together.

There is also nothing nonexistent about my own Soviet Union, about the predicament and constant awareness of being born into one geopolitical reality in the world and then being snapped without warning into a wholly foreign and oppositional geopolitical reality. There is something very real about my bicultural experience of the Cold War, of the conviction that my parents had into the post-Soviet 1990s that Russian tanks were on the verge of rolling across Europe. For example, on the day in April 1986 when the United States bombed Libya, my parents (they deny this now) woke me up for school letting me know that World War III was likely to begin, that Soviet Union would most certainly retaliate, that everyone was done for. While I don't have a poem on this topic, I remember scrutinizing a world map that day in a sincere attempt to find yet another country for us to immigrate to, as far away as possible from the global catastrophe I was told to anticipate: the poems in *My Soviet Union* frequently pivot from one geographic locale to another, fueled by a pre-apocalyptic apprehension analogous to the confusion and anxiety I felt that morning.

There is likewise nothing nonexistent about my lifelong hyperconsciousness of the inaccessible alternate reality I would have lived had my parents been denied permission to emigrate, of the awareness that Mikhail Edouardovich Dumanis of Moscow is a very different person than the person I became, that I will never know him, and yet, paradoxically, that I will always experience the world through his eyes. And this is what I, however elliptically, find myself writing about all of the time—contradictory realities and versions of childhood, place and displacement, a sense that my speaker is standing in front of the smoldering ruins of an empire, the instability and slippages of language, being snapped back and forth between situations and worlds.

One other thing troubles me about the reviewer's assertion: this idea that simply because my English-language poems are perhaps influenced in their choices of idiom and dramatic situation, approaches to enjambment, and narrative strategies by some of the American poets I study and particularly love—for instance, John Berryman, Mark Strand, Heather McHugh, Lucie Brock-Broido, Michael Palmer, Olena Kalytiak Davis, and Dean Young—that I am a wholly American poet, whatever that means. My sense of what a poem was, what it could be used for and what it could do to another person, began with my mother reading her own poem to me when I was five years old.

The role of poetry in Russian culture is different than the role of poetry in American culture. Ex-Soviets of my parents' age know

multiple poems by heart—they tend to see them as tools for express-
ing emotions and contextualizing complex situations. Because their
generation had no freedom, they saw in words more than their mere
denotations. They were always looking for subtext, for ways to communicate through nuance and word play and allusion and metaphor.
While I was growing up, my father would interrupt (and derail) many
a dinner conversation by abruptly heading to the bookshelf, locating
a volume of poetry, finding a particular page he thought relevant,
and proceeding to emphatically and passionately share it. I grew up
assuming that this happened at all dinner tables in all countries, that
poetry had an intrinsic value as a potential reference point and source
of wisdom in the most routine of conversations, that the books of
poems my parents had shipped over from the USSR were somehow
indispensable to the understanding and processing of daily life.

The poetry in my parents' books, which ranged from collections of
Mayakovsky and Mandelstam to rhymey, jingoistic Socialist Realist
verse by Soviet poets who died in the Second World War—tended to
be wildly declarative and loud in its rhythms, attentive to its surfaces,
dramatic in its content, ambitious in its tackling of heady subjects
and big themes. This poetry was a poetry meant to be read loudly,
breathlessly, full-throttle, full of sonic energy and internal rhyme. It
felt less like a communication from a speaker to a reader and more
like sheet music for a reader to perform with their own voice. The
Russian language has more flexibility with syntax than English and
I have always gravitated to American poets who delight in upending
the natural order of words. So I grew up to write American poetry
animated by American English and frequently set in a recognizably
American landscape, yet wholly rooted in Russian language and tradition, composed with a distinctly Russian ear and what I think is a
distinctly Soviet, ex-Soviet, or would-be-Soviet sensibility.

II: Language

What Language Are You?

Andrei Guruianu

> For a writer's language, far from being a mere means of
> expression, is above all a mode of subjective existence and a
> way of experiencing the world. She needs the language not just
> to describe things, but to *see* them. [...] A writer's language
> is not just something she uses, but a constitutive part of what
> she is. This is why to abandon your native tongue and to adopt
> another is to dismantle yourself, piece by piece, and then to put
> yourself together again, in a different form.
> —Costica Bradatan, "Born Again in a Second Language",
> *New York Times*

As an immigrant writer in America, who has largely abandoned his
native language, I sometimes feel as if I'm playing my own character,
the embodiment of an "I" whom everyone watches from a distance
but who is nothing more than a flimsy façade. "Someone is living my
life," wrote the Sicilian playwright Luigi Pirandello in his diary, not
long before his death. "And I don't know a thing about him." Sometimes, though, when performing a walk-through of my own play, I
truly believe in my own act, as if it weren't an illusion. But it doesn't
take much to blur the lines. When strangers ask me to say something
in Romanian, or to explain why I no longer write in the "old language," I feel as if I'm asked to perform yet again, to prove myself or

to play the expected role. I don't blame them. People want to know: How much of an immigrant are you? If you really are Romanian, present your calling card—the words, the language, the accent.

Because I've been in America long enough, I am no longer aware of the language I use when I write or speak, the way I used to be when I first transitioned from Romanian to English. Unfailingly, though, someone always manages to remind me. Even the most casual query can make me self-conscious. I am reminded of an NPR interview with Nancy Cartwright, the actress best known as the voice of Bart Simpson, where she discussed the baggage that comes with being an iconic character. She said that the most common request she gets from people is to "Do Bart!" Most of the time, Cartwright humors them with the phrase "Eat my shorts!" or "Don't have cow, man!" But as soon as these words escape her mouth, she explained, Bart's voice becomes her "real" voice while her natural voice becomes "fake."

For the immigrant or exile, this bizarre ventriloquism is not a career but a necessity. We are asked to perform (freely or otherwise) to better adapt to circumstance. The number of years away from our homeland hardly matter. Acting has become second nature, an ingrained mechanism, to the extent that the lines can become so blurred that one can no longer distinguish between past and present. Instead, the two form a twisted but continuous loop called reality. This Möbius strip is the permanent immigrant condition.

The paradox of the Möbius strip, a two-dimensional sheet with only one surface, points to the difference between Eastern and Western thought. Western thought, rigid and set in its ways, enforces delineations. Certain laws shall not be broken. That's just the way things are. Eastern thought, which allows for flexibility and continuity, is less structured but still disciplined. Exile is endurance training in finding a middle ground that can be inhabited between the two. Ultimately, we learn to accept that the old ways of thinking might not necessarily work anymore. Rigidity defines monuments but life demands flexibility.

Subsequently, as the alien begins taking on roots in a new language, he also learns to bend and negotiate, to compromise and improvise. Transience and contingency require a Zen practice, but this rarely leads to bliss and enlightenment. Few things are more painfully unnatural than "naturalization." By necessity, then, all immigrants live in a kind of permanent exile, whether self-imposed or otherwise. No gain comes without a loss. That much is obvious, and that much is made certain by the necessity of living between worlds where the border between past and present, old and new selves, is always being redefined. Under such conditions, life becomes a constant haggle with customs inspectors.

All they require, thankfully, is the secret password. When on cue I say "*Ce faci?*" (How are you?) or "*Bine ai venit*" (Welcome) to someone who wants to hear what Romanian sounds like, a secret gate seems to swing open and I finally appear as a concrete being, albeit one with a pre-defined and pre-loaded label—which, because it is reduced to a known quantity, is rendered familiar and therefore harmless. In other words, I become a copy of a copy that someone remembers seeing once on a PBS special, that paragon of cultural dissemination. Luckily, if you missed it, there are repeats, or TiVo. And every time the special plays, we multiply but remain exactly the same, charged with the preservation of an image of history, culture on late-night parade—the projection of an identity marked and fixed by signifiers.

In the end, that is the biggest lie the exile is forced to tell, and it always begins with "I am ..." As easy and as painful as pulling an old line out of a tired repertoire performed to indulgent applause. In those moments, whether Cartwright performs Bart or Guruianu performs Andrei, both she and I become someone else. She is no longer Nancy, mother of two. She is not even a Primetime Emmy winning voice actress playing an iconic pop character. She *is* Bart Simpson, an animated 10-year-old boy, more real to most adult viewers than their own middle-school children.

Likewise, through my own voice-over, I become—to a large extent and to the exclusion of everything else—a cartoon immigrant, a two-dimensional foreigner. Amit Majmudar, in his *New York Times* opinion piece "Am I an 'Immigrant Writer'", puts it this way:

> Notice how many celebrated minority writers of our time—
> Mr. Díaz, Chimamanda Ngozi Adichie, Jhumpa Lahiri—tend
> to write inside their own communities. One explanation
> may well be the nature of realism, which is (for now) literary
> fiction's dominant mode: the artistic need for observed detail,
> and the tendency of literary novelists to tweak their personal
> experiences into fiction.
>
> Write what you know, young writers are taught. This may
> well reinforce, and be reinforced by, our sense of a writer's
> being an authority only on his or her own community, his or
> her own people.
>
> So, in a paradoxical way, the freedom to write about your
> own experience turns into a restriction on the subject matter
> permissible to you. Your selling point governs how you are
> perceived.

Should I choose not to play by those rules, what might I lose? Should I choose to play the game, what have I already lost? Either way, we all seem to need better representation. That's the only way to survive show biz.

The Language of my Desire

Cristián Flores García

I am growing a language. Still, after twenty years of having been transplanted, I find myself in constant translation.

My languages are native. I was born into Spanish. I thrived in a land of Aztec history, in a borough know as the "place of coyotes," where poverty was everybody's mother and hope was our Huitzilopochtli. Thirteen years later I was transposed into the dry, Southern Californian English of which I understood *hello, chicken, pen, table,* and *window,* thanks to the grace of a song learned back in third grade. I was delivered and lost within the immensity of a code yet to unravel.

I was reborn. I had to learn to eat the foods that smelled and looked and tasted different to what I was accustomed to. I had to learn to walk comfortably on deserted, clean streets, without fear of petty crime, though fearing police because of the shade of my skin, with my head down and avoiding all possible eye contact, always looking over my shoulder without smiling in celebration of my existence as I always did in the place where I was born. Though my body was of a teenager, my mind was infant; figuring out by the minute, the day, months, and years the arithmetic of a new language: nouns or pronouns, plus verbs, and adjectives or adverbs, plus prepositions, conjunctions, and/or interjections equals the expression of a need or desire.

In both lives I read almost never. And when I read I read without any passion. In both of my lives the only books we owned were the Bible and the first two of a ten-tome encyclopedia. In both lives I was always hungry and my mind loaded with thoughts of dishes I craved constantly. I read English understanding mostly prepositions and necessary common verbs for the first five years or so of my new life. My vocabulary bloomed slowly. And yet I was able to totter my way to the university ranks. Because of my need of English to survive I abandoned all but the conversational form of Spanish.

I chose to attend university to feel as though I was going somewhere with my life, though I went from day to day with scant fervor for anything other than family. One day poetry was a requirement. I was in a class to gain credits to move onto the next, and the next, and so forth. That first night, of that spring quarter, I went home and opened the book to find, *The whiskey on your breath / Could make a small boy dizzy;* and I hung onto this image. For the first time I was alive in English. I had arrived at feeling. In the instant the words entered me I thought of my own father. There was only feeling; no translating, no imagining, there was no mental blackout. There was inclusion. It was I, germinating. Change was inevitable.

Poetry wasn't linear. Poetry was breakage. Poetry was like my thoughts, fragmented and winding. I discovered poetry in English and as I flipped the pages and read more poems I felt embraced even when I didn't understand a word, a phrase, or an idea. Poetry gave me English. English gave me poetry. *I love you* was the first expression I exchanged with my sister in English without stopping to think what it meant, we were on the phone and after it sprout from my lips there was a silence. It was as if both she and I were paying tribute to the death of a fundamental root only to attach our selves to a new one. The shame of speaking fragmented and accented English started to vanish. The seed of poetry was planted and I knew only that in poetry I felt safe. I had the comfort of Spanish waiting at home and the excitement of a new affair in my newly unleashed English. Becoming a poet was a horizon I wanted to reach. It was poetry that woke up my desire to learn. It was poetry that woke up my desire to show others what it was like to be a foreigner. It was poetry the tool I could comfort others with. With poetry I could praise and celebrate those dear to me. Poetry gave life to my bilingual life. In poetry I created the language of my desire, mixing Spanish and English as I thought, felt, wrote, and spoke. To be a poet in America meant inclusion; inclusion into history, inclusion to joys and pains, inclusion into many lives. Poetry was and remains the greatest affair between my languages and me. Poetry is the language growing within me as I grow within America, and language is the moment in which I find myself living.

In The Name Of The Letter, The Spirit & The Double Helix

Fady Joudah

1.

In the beginning there was translation. Without it there's no expression, not even gene expression, no life. Even the untranslatable is functional, vital for the process. To splice one must first excise. Memory, with its trident of recall, imagination and transformation is translation's muse and taxonomy. Memory is sometimes unconscious cognition, other times absence. In an integrative age, grid and matrix rename the prongs, erect isomers or chiasms, employ catalog, entropy or the enzymatic for reproduction's sake. Not all creation is equal. We're not all butterflies. Meaning burns us as we burn it. Our predilection is replication and mimicry.

2.

"But before that where were you born?" Like an anchor I was born a sleeper. I pulled myself up to a boat, lived on railroad tracks until I was returned to light, awash in a cell. My polygraph included rapid fill-in-the-blanks that asked for prepositions, autocorrect my alibi. An essay's infrared portion droned my antecedental clarity. My semicolon was semicomma. Congruence was entrapped between intransitive terminals as the flight was rendered on time's time, a hyperlink to a link, a biography in Facebook movements. Before boarding, on YouTube, a man and a woman crossed water on wireless fidelity. They were afraid of being left behind like some orphaned refugee siblings in the mayhem of survival. Adrenaline or endorphin is the original music score. They had four children. The youngest was a boy, the eldest a girl, maybe ten years old, and the middle two were twins, zygosity notwithstanding. The eldest got her siblings through the journey then died of a depression that commanded her language back to nature, her immunity not to speak when spoken to.

3.

The most astonishing recurrence in human narrative remains that of the displaced. Between the word body and the world body we are shadows of health and nation, teratology and homelessness, infestation and cohabitation, the sacred as the accursed. How do you say "May you wake up to a country" in one language and make it sound like "sleep tight" in another? Are we still the same since the days of Homer and Mo? Was Brecht right when he said at the House of Un-American Activities that "ideas of how to make use of the new capabilities of production have not been much developed since the days horse had to do what man could not do"? One must believe in evolution, a way out of mind in it.

4.

Expression can reach tyrosine kinase overdrive. (T/F)
Prose is as impossible as poetry after the Congo. (T/F)
By the time of Andrew Jackson, the last of the Conquistadors, there were no microbes left for the natives. (T/F)

Normal thought occurs irregularly. (T/F)
The soul is an epigenetic of quantum mechanics. (T/F)
Sometimes the poem is permitted to go to a field of action. (T/F)
What can't be proven is true only when uncertainty is in agreement
with measurement. (T/F)

5.

Through meiosis, a shuffle of genes, a recombinant crossover into
diversity, we establish filiation. Meiosis is not a cycle but a reduc-
tion in preparation for reproduction, a lessening before the thread.
Poetry is not incest. Filiation moves into affiliation, which moves
through mitosis to culture and system, a machinery of reliable
reproducibility. If culture is in the business of "possessing possession" then system is its dream of "camouflaging jargon." Autoim-
mune diatribe, debris of aura's disintegration, "jargon's constant
invective against reification is itself reified." Poetry is not empire.
Whether meiotic or mitotic the secret ingredient must first be
unzipped for the messenger. As Eros occurs, errors occur. Often
deleterious, mutations can be advantageous. Between culture and
system, in the codons unrepaired, bypassed or abandoned by the
impossible desire for precise control, poetry is resistance, a critical
consciousness of "noncoercive knowledge produced in the interests
of human freedom."

6.

False eloquence argues opposite sides of a cause with equal force.
Autonomous and committed poetry become autonomic. Time
stands invisible while a canon enlists skilled labor to manufacture
its inevitability. The center mercurially centers itself into peripher-

ies. It cannot hold, it holds, "a negation of negation," a reterritorialization of deterritorialization. When one's conception is not that of a literature of masters, the masters will show up driving their fiats. Meanwhile, in the waiting room, a smooth Kenny G tune is playing a spa footnote in history, what one desires as more than what one becomes. The reactionary, whether restorative or obliterative, is soon a tool for the totalitarian. This is not what Sufis meant by "when all opposites are one." They were standing outside language in it.

7.

A poet's hypothesis to needle-graph one's cranial sutures then translate the results into each of the five senses remains untested. Could an electropoeticogram (EPG) be a poet's filiative thumbprint into the world, a fossil record of his or her primary emotions? Then what? Arabic poetry "in which the five senses seem to have a more simultaneous and equal share," a Bacchian Zarathustrian fantasy, becomes an antecedent "supernatural" prescience of the neuroscientific image. Pound the Chinese. Occam's fighting for his life.

8.

So far image in neuroscience is the principal "web of relationships" in the mind, a "movie in the brain." Beyond the visual and "with as many sensory tracks as there are sensory portals" "the self comes to mind in the form of images, relentlessly telling a story of such engagements." Yet an "explanatory gap" persists. All we see is evidence of interaction. One is unable to watch the mind watch the self in action. Surveillance is not total. If that day ever comes both mind and self would have evolved new secrets.

9.

The revolutionary tradition and its lost treasure announce their closure parenthetically. The criterion of equality and the principle of authority in arts are necessarily "conspicuously absent." "The rank of a poet, for instance is decided neither by a vote of confidence of his fellow poets nor by fiat coming from the recognized master, but by those who only love poetry and are incapable of ever writing a line." In which age is this true? The jury, those only-incapable-lovers are currently an endangered species. Their preservation aims at their conscription into fields of action, reservations held and built in advance, whose cancellation carries a threat of exile, expatriation, and extradition. A work of art that posits itself outside tradition may not leave a thread behind to lead to it, out of the labyrinth of oblivion. A task for poets is to inventory memory, search for collective enunciation and guard against a freedom from politics.

10.

Evolutionary technology is "breaking the glass ceiling of attention."
(T/F)
If homeostasis is the backdrop, thought is the rhythm of sea brine.
(T/F)
Ritalin paste is the new shock experience. (T/F)
Poetry outside capital on MRI screens gives off no signals. (T/F)
Signs price the known at the expense of the unknowable. (T/F)
By the next century one will be able to download intuition. (T/F)
"So long as you say 'one' instead of 'I' there's nothing in it." (T/F)

11.

It's 9:38 AM. I am juggling a fat cat grant, spinning my metaphase spindles on the category of submission to the fellowship of the ring.

It's a day off, one of many I've worked hard to secure for my better writing and non-writing self. Alone I go to the movies, 11:05 AM show, Fruitvale Station in Trayvon Martin American days. The Native American is the first to be forgotten, the last to remember our proliferative loyalty tests. Hierarchy of suffering, you can have your crumbs and eat them too. Reparation is law, law is king, the king is dead, long live the king.

12.

I knew a grandma like that once in American borderlands. She grew too large after some asshole doctor left her on steroid pills for so long, lost to follow-up, a no-show like show-business I know. It's not illegal not to explain the treatment plan, fear to hope and hope to fear. Click here, electronic medical record. After some lost weight and partial regain of function, walker et al, we found out that grandma had breast cancer. By we I mean she, then I, then the biopsy crew. The land of mass is the land of mass displacement is impossible to name. She willed herself to die before chemo began.

13.

Here it is again the "woman as symptom," "another tragedy in a long line of low-rent tragedies." Sometimes one gives birth to novels, screenplays, poems, symposia, scholarly "toilsome idleness," even doctors without borders. Good is never good enough is never enough of it around. Forgery of the true body begins when one forgets how to die. As if dying comes with a manual and living, as a teenager once told me, is the longest thing you'll ever do. Love is not one of the primary emotions. Testimony is love the way compassion is a temporary visa to forgetfulness.

14.

Each author has several doubles. The difference between the true author and the real one is the latter's legitimate counterfeit. This has been the rule of market since the days of Jahiz. "Every genre is buoyed by those names that alone can grant admission to a new text." One must carry at least one diagnosis as "a sort of homage rendered to a past studded with prestigious authors whose examples—whose discourse—must be perpetuated." A real author is also "the principle of thrift in the proliferation of meaning." The past is a trans-splicing oncogene. The past is apoptosis of apoptosis, controlled death of programmed death, divinity as tumorous benignity. Poets create analogies, not difference. Between poetry and discursivity is science.

15.

The science of ancient Greece is a science of religion, a Lazarus of language. It has latched itself to carbon and half-life, nouveau decay to extend the imperial aesthetic. "Fascism aims at nothing less than the commandeering of myth." The song of self is a swan song but the swan is miles high. Descent begins in microgravity, a power of endless endings. Not weightlessness exactly, but the way a body at rest tends to stay in motion within an inertial frame of reference whose speed is imperceptible. The past is not always lost. Its replacement is not always necessary. Reconstitution is sometimes syndrome or revenge.

16.

"I broke myth and I broke," "I want from love only the beginning," love at last sight. If speechlessness is "the great sorrow of nature," then love is a triumphal song of naming. If it is "a metaphysical truth that all nature would begin to lament if it were endowed with language" then "if olive trees knew the hands that had planted them, their oil would turn to tears." A true poet dreams of the regression of poetry. I don't mean a "silken boredom" where a mad race for invention would "bear amiss the second burden of a former child." True regression of poetry is tightly linked to true progress of humanity. Meanwhile, déjà vu falls between overnaming and eternal repetition. In the explanatory gap, love moves as an echo. Evolution is not domination. *Who am I* (not *Aren't I*) that is the question.

The essay is partly based on the writings of several authors who are either paraphrased or directly quoted or both. These authors are G. Vico, M. Darwish, J. Baldwin, E. Said, T. Adorno, G. Deleuze, Rilke, A. Dimasio, H. Arendt, Kafka, J. Rose, R. Carver, C. G. Jochmann, A. Kilito, M. Foucault, W. Benjamin, Shakespeare.

Like a Bear Playing a Flute
Piotr Gwiazda

The necessity of carving out [intuiting/enacting] one's own
treatment of a particular arena of language
—Myung Mi Kim, *Commons*

The challenge of writing in English, my second language, has been central to my identity as a poet. I moved from Poland to the United States at the age of seventeen; I was "naturalized" six years later. So it seemed only "natural" for me to choose English. Although I had begun writing poems in Poland, and even managed to publish some of them in literary magazines, I don't remember having any serious doubts about my decision. Or was it just the mad rush to assimilate? In any event, since my arrival in America writing in English has always been for me a matter of practical as well as artistic necessity.

If, as many believe, poetic ability or sensibility originates in the unconscious, in the "forgotten," or at least in early childhood, writing in an adoptive language seems like an insuperable task. George Santayana, born and raised in Spain, once explained why he could never call himself as an English-language poet: "I never drank in in childhood the homely cadences and ditties which in pure spontaneous poetry set the essential key." Paul Celan, who wrote in German but lived in Paris, said: "Only in the mother tongue can one speak one's own truth. In a foreign tongue the poet lies." Czesław Miłosz, who paid homage to the Polish language in his poem "My Faithful Mother Tongue," states on a number of occasions that true dialogue between poets and their audience can only exist within a shared language and literary tradition. I can provide several more statements, which I have been assiduously collecting over the years, that make pretty much the same point.

The best way I can describe my own relationship with the English language is by quoting Santayana again: "Its roots do not quite reach my center." The relationship is surely somewhat artificial and tenuous, since the language I write in doesn't come from "within." But it is also dynamic, evolving, intense; sometimes I'm tempted to call it lover-like. It probably has a deeply psychological aspect to it, as I made the switch at the threshold of adulthood. At the very least, it makes me acutely aware of the illusion of personal autonomy vis-à-vis the culture and (ultimately) the language any individual is born into. Celan once said to his friend Yves Bonnefoy: "You are at home within your language, your reference points, among the books, the works you love. As for me, I am on the outside." He was referring, of course, to the isolation of writing in his mother tongue while living in France. (The German language was also, as his biographer John Felstiner puts it, "his mother's murderers' tongue.") But the idea of being "on the outside" —being displaced, whether linguistically or culturally, and so unable to take one's medium for granted—seems to me central to the idea of poetry as such. One has to accept a certain level of alienation in one's life, *from* one's life, in order to inhabit that other, exclusively verbal realm. After all, what is a poem if not a personal act of attention to language? All poets, to some extent, are *alone* with their language—whether it's their first or second or third language.

These days much attention is paid to the phenomenon of literature written in the author's foreign language—the so-called "exo-

phonic" writing. This is not surprising, given how many contemporary writers operate in transnational and/or translinguistic settings.
For example, in her recent book *Unoriginal Genius*, Marjorie Perloff
discusses the work of Yoko Tawada (among others), a Japanese-born
writer who lives in Berlin and writes in German and who popular-
ized the term "exophony" in the early 2000s. The term signifies a
merging of two linguistic strata that can produce unique variations
of syntax, diction, rhythm, accent, and so on. The result is a kind
of defamiliarization one usually expects in poetic writing, but in
a manner that makes the *absence* of the writer's native language
somehow palpable in the text. Perloff states flat out that writing in
a second language is a major constraint—and she is right. But the
whole point of her study is to show how writers work around self-
imposed constraints as part of their experimentation with language.
(After all, writing in one's native language can be viewed as a limitation also.) In this context, it is useful to invoke Samuel Beckett who
once justified his decision to abandon English in favor of French
by citing "the need to be ill equipped" (*le besoin d'être mal armé*—a
likely pun on Mallarmé). It seems that Beckett began to write in
French for the sake of estrangement, as though to enter into a more
unfamiliar, antagonistic, *poetic* relationship with the medium.

Exophonic writers like Beckett are often described as being
equally fluent in their native and their adoptive language. But I suspect this is not quite true; few people can boast exactly the same kind
of facility in two languages. Besides, the concept of fluency is relative. What does it mean to actually *know* a language, let alone master
a language, especially if we consider the difference between writing
and speaking? The point, in any case, is not fluency or mastery, but
an essential *feel* for the second language, a physical instinct for its
rhythms and idioms. "There is an inherent clumsiness about this,

like a bear playing a flute, that is embarrassing," said John Bayley
in his review of Joseph Brodsky's book of poems written in English
So Forth. This statement should give pause to anyone who intends
to write poems in his or her adoptive language. It certainly gave *me*
pause when I first read it in 1996, though at the same time it made
me wonder about the creative possibilities of bilingualism. Can the
imperfect grasp of the language in which one writes—what special-
ists call linguistic interference—ever lead to artistic discovery? Can
being literally "ill equipped"—not having the comfort of writing
in one's mother tongue—ever prove aesthetically interesting? How
does writing in an adoptive language help one defamiliarize that
language—similar to the way nonnative, nonstandard pronuncia-
tion sometimes becomes "song added to speech" (which is what the
word "accent" etymologically signifies)?

Even so, as Friedrich Schleiermacher says in his celebrated essay
on translation, "what one produces in a foreign tongue is not original." Since I abandoned my mother tongue twenty years ago, I have
certainly experienced the peculiar mixture of solitude and disori-
entation that comes from the consciousness of being removed from
both one's native *and* one's adopted culture. I have also long ago
resigned myself to the fact that I will never be able to pass for a
native speaker or writer of English. At the same time, I don't want
to depict my situation in such irretrievably tragic terms, especially if they presuppose relatively static conceptions of language,
nationality, and identity. If a poem is an act of personal attention
to language, it is at the same time a very public act, a manifestation
of the mind in conversation with itself. In ways I myself can only
partly describe, the poems I have written and still hope to write are
a product of my linguistic difference, my barbarian sensibility—and
that is perhaps their own kind of truth. Plastic poems of a plastic

person? If so, these poems are also a reflection of the basic facts of my biography—growing up in Poland, coming to the United States in my teenage years, living in different American cities for the last two and a half decades as an unassimilated citizen. No matter how foreign my poems may appear to those who read them, I would like to think that they implicitly tell a story of not only my giving up of one language for another but giving myself *over* to a new language and the ways it shapes my experience of the world. Regardless of how hard I try to make them my own, I hope that they will always remain translations without an original.

English as a Second Language

Vasyl Makhno

Translated from Ukrainian by Ostap Kin and Ali Kinsella

Everyone who comes to the United States legally, that is, following all the rules for crossing the American border, has the opportunity to study or improve his English by signing up for various courses at colleges and universities. The course that the American educational system offers newcomers is called "English as a Second Language," and it's primarily taught by native speakers. Frankly speaking, they have only a superficial grasp of how to teach, if they get it at all, so the results of such studies aren't great. Better classes (and, accordingly, instructors) at good universities are usually expensive, and "new Americans" can't afford them. Therefore hundred of thousands of new immigrants pass through these courses all over the United States, because everyone—if culture shock hasn't completely fogged up her thinking—on some level, conscious or unconscious, understands that, without English, it's game over. After achieving some proficiency in vocabulary and in syntactical constructions, mixing up plurals and singulars and the present tense with past, pronouncing words with one accent or another, they all dash headlong into this English-speaking ocean with hopes of swimming it out, that is, surviving.

I was looking for a deeper subtext in the course's title, "English as a Second Language," because for a person who writes, who creates

texts in a language other than English, English will always remain
second, and the culture which one inhabits will also be second or
different. Perhaps writers from countries where English never dominated (for we weren't all British colonies like India or Bangladesh),
have always felt English to be a second language, although everyone
has his own experience of studying and using it: Czesław Miłosz
taught and wrote articles in English, but his poetry was written in
Polish; Joseph Brodsky taught in English and wrote both essays and
poems, but his English poetry does not compare to his Russian; Josef
Škvorecký, in Canada, wrote his novels in Czech; David Albakhari,
in that same Canada, writes in Serbian; Anna Frajlich writes her
verses in Polish; Marko Robert Stech writes his prose in Ukrainian.
I'm talking about people who moved to a new world at a mature
age and, for a variety of reasons, didn't switch to English in their
writings (by the way, Škvorecký and Albakhari studied English at
the universities of Prague and Belgrade), and remained on the borderlands, predominantly on the borderlands of languages. Yet, as
Dorota Masłowska ironically notes, today even Europe is a place
where everyone speaks English.

I read something that struck me as not quite accurate in a Ukrainian magazine that published a piece on me: "The Ukrainian, but
now American, writer Vasyl Makhno." I smiled and ordered coffee
because I was actually sitting in my favorite Starbucks. After surfing
through several webpages, I started traveling across America, examining different states, especially the exotic Nevada, Texas, Arkansas,
and Kansas, and then switched to fish as if I were interested in fish
the most…

But outside the window, which revealed Third Avenue to me, was
New York itself. I wanted to compare its hectic, variegated, and restless rhythm with music. Directly across from me, on the opposite

side of Eighth Street—known as Saint Mark's Place—a saxophonist
stood like a post. For some reason he spent a long time shining his
mouthpiece with a velvet cloth. He was getting ready to play, but in
any case I wouldn't be able to hear him, sitting here at Starbucks: in
the end, I would have to wait until someway entered from the street
or left the café. Then, for a second, the open door would allow a
snippet of one of the saxophonist's phrases to charge into the room,
interrupting the monotonous country music that had already been
playing for two hours. Yes, I'd been sitting in this damned place for
two good hours! Dusk began to fall; the streetlights slowly came on.
Finally, the guy tucked the cloth into his case, licked his lips with his
red tongue, and started playing. For a long time, no one entered or
left the coffee shop. Country music was replaced by some jazz. The
street musician practiced the gymnastics of the body and twirled
the silver instrument in his hands in vain—I couldn't hear him. It
was like turning off the sound and watching a silent movie. I began
to wonder how long it would last. A few minutes later, two students
entered the café and brought with them not only the music, but also
the smell and sound of the street. I thanked the two flighty girls in
my mind, and they started excitedly discussing the forthcoming
party that they were going to attend.

I've long been convinced that landscape is something more than
just one of nuisances that causes visual impressions. I dreamed of living in a city where the landscape would consist of a sea or an ocean,
of seagulls and yachts. But yachts and seagulls aren't the only things
that come into your consciousness when you live near the ocean: a
new language becomes a more important factor uniting your new
streets and avenues into a whole and muffling the squawks of seagulls
with its music. Which is to say, this is that part of the landscape that
is simultaneously a struggle with language and with seagulls.

Yet in all of this—that is, in all the doubts about the expediency of language and cultural borderlands—the very act of *being* triumphs: *creating, writing, uttering, reading, defeating,* and *overcoming* yourself, and resisting other cultures, other languages, other mentalities, other landscapes; this is, so to speak, all on the one hand. On the other, there is studying this *otherness*, and trying to unite that which is yours and that which is *other* like a zipper joins two halves of a coat.

Of course, you can console yourself with the illusion that the very circumstances of your life aren't all that essential, and the preservation of poetic language, in your case, is more important than the creation of that language's universality for a direct rivalry with English. It's also possible to stamp out the feeling within of being on the edge, on the borderland, but that would also be a terribly erroneous move.

There's a lot you can do!

Several years ago, I happened to accidentally attend a book release party for a new collection of poetry by a New York poet R. I received an invitation that told me what it was and what it was for, as well as the address (West 14th St.); the small postcard with its golden edge reminded me of the paintings on Chinese porcelain. Having arrived early at the indicated address, I murmured something like "Did you have book party today?" and they said something in return. The owner of the unpleasant voice on the intercom happened to be the nice-looking hostess and editor of a New York-based publishing house. What shocked me most was that she and her family lived in a loft—a former factory with twenty-foot ceilings and an indecent total square footage, so big that it was hardly noticeable when the gathering had grown to fifty people. On a little table in the enormous room that served as the living room there was a small heap of the recently published collection; the price was handwritten on a white card to the side—$20. In another room, drinks and snacks stood on a long table: mainly nuts, chips, and dips. The hosts sat me down on a leather sofa and quickly forgot about me as the guests started to arrive. The typical greetings sounded—"Hi, how are you?" or "Nice to meet you"—the shaking of hands, laughter, jokes. It was strange that I couldn't at first figure out who was guilty of organizing the event; the books lay about the table by their lonesome: someone might pick one up with interest, flip through it, and put it back. Later, at the height of the reception, when I was standing in line to refill my glass of wine and toss some more chips onto my disposable plate, someone tugged me by the arm and introduced me to the author. We smiled at each other and then calmly turned away, he to his group and I to my chips.

Several groups formed in the living room. One group of young people sat on the floor around an ashtray, silently smoking and drinking wine and beer; others, also with an ashtray, stood by the window that looked out onto an evening in Union Square and loudly discussed some article in *The New Yorker*. Since I had run out of cigarettes (back then I still smoked), my most pressing task was to find a victim who would share a smoke. It seemed like it would be easy, although it's pretty impossible to bum a cigarette on a New York street on your first try. In my experience, no matter what country they live in, smokers really cherish their boyfriends and girlfriends. So right after taking the two slim cigarettes immediately proffered me by a young person with a pierced nose and an Italian designer skirt, I headed to another windowsill, settled in, and smoked.

I had a feeling of loneliness, strengthened by the increasingly stronger awareness of the unnecessariness of this party, of these puny, stoned Americans, these shitty intellectuals, these books, and these poems. Behind my back people shouted, smoked, laughed, squawked, broke their wineglasses, put burns in the high-quality leather sofa and the disposable plates with their cigarette butts, and discussed their articles and poems, while in front of me pulsed the worn rhythm of New York at night.

I stubbed out the cigarette and left without saying anything to anyone.

My absence, I hope, went unnoticed.

During these seven years in the United States, I've read quite often to Ukrainian and American audiences. I've signed books, answered questions, participated in Slavic conferences, traveled to Europe to read at poetry festivals, given interviews to numerous publications in different languages, and met with many writers of the world and people far from literature and art.

I published several books. I started writing essays and plays. I quit smoking, and I bought a car.

There's a lot that I started and a lot that I quit. Now I make fun of myself, of this bookkeeping; I was always afraid of accounting courses.

One time the Ukrainian émigré poet Bohdan Rubchak and I touched upon the topic of *bifurcation* in the sense that, after ending up in the West, a writer, especially one from Eastern, post-communist Europe, is indisputably a *bifurcated* person. (Bohdan Boychuk's return to Kyiv is also a bifurcation, just in the other direction.) This subject brought us to another no less important topic in our dialogue: the interrelationship between the genuinely Ukrainian and the diaspora or émigré, this constant conflict between what is *ours, native, homegrown, we-are-ourselves-Europe,* and what is offered (of course, the best examples) by all waves of immigration and the Ukrainianness all around—and their offerings are not meager:

Archipenko (in sculpture), the New York Group (in literature), Shevelov (in linguistics), Fizer, Rubchak, Grabowicz (in literary studies). I will limit myself to that which is closest and that which is in one way or another directed at Ukraine. But the paradox is that *homegrown Europe* doesn't need this. With minor exceptions, it is all either cast aside or distorted; that is, this unique experience, based on global norms, is simply whistled away by buffoons.

The next time I'm asked what it means to *be a Ukrainian poet in America*, I want to answer right away with a question: *and what does it mean to be a Ukrainian poet in Ukraine?* America at least doesn't care what language your poetry is in, and doesn't demand any acknowledgement. In Ukraine, I believe, there's an illusion that poetry and the poet are needed, because they might study you in school and write about you in the encyclopedia. The new Ukrainian bourgeoisie show off their cars, watches, suits, and shoes online, but they couldn't give two shits about Ukrainian poetry, these refined aesthetes who are obsessively eager to sell themselves to the nouveau riche—for a decent price, of course. And it's not even worth talking about politicians … We're somehow missing the main thing that sets poetry apart from life. What's the point of all this practice in combining words which we partially call poetry, prose, etc., if we're just driving ourselves into the dead end of modernity and cannot answer a simple question: *If art is a game, then to what degree does this realization allow us to adequately consider everything connected with it?*

I'd like to conclude my deliberations on the right to choose as a human right in this new, globalized, and no less tragic time, where I started—with music.

In the Toronto subway, I was once stopped by the Russian song "Moscow Nights" being played by a dwarf on balalaika; I paused and tossed a few Canadian coins into the wide-open beak of his case, on which the word "Kiev" was clearly written. I asked him in Ukrainian: "Where are you from?" "I'm from Kyiv, from the Kyiv circus." We chatted a bit about various unimportant things, accompanied by the rumble of the subway, and at the very end he said with some sorrow, "You know, the local Ukrainians don't accept me because I play the balalaika. Even when I play Ukrainian tunes…"

I sympathized with him and we bade each other farewell. I was grateful that his balalaika had stopped me so we could exchange a few words, two wanderers in this world. When I was already exiting, the feeble sounds of a Ukrainian melody my new acquaintance was playing caught up to me. I understood that this melody was especially for me, and I thanked him in my mind.

III: Influences

Institutionalized
My Influences as an American Poet
Gerardo Pacheco Matus

I am Mayan, Mexican, Latino, Hispanic, Immigrant, Undocumented, Illegal, Wet-back, Greaser, Mojado, and so many more
adjectives you may think of. Most importantly, I am a writer, a poet
living in the United States of America.

I write with a point of view of an undocumented immigrant in
the United States of America. I write as a man trying to understand
my role in the creative writing world. I am trying to understand
where I belong, and who I am as a writer. I write in order to discover
my "past" and "heritage."

As a graduate student, one of my professors brought to my attention that I was "institutionalized" that I was "stacked in the past,
where only the dead writers dwell." My professor meant well of
course. Every time, this professor would ask me who my influences
were? Or who were the writers that motivated me to write poetry?
I always answered that William Shakespeare, Christopher Marlow,
and even Ovid have had a great influence in my poetry. These are
the western, canonized, male writers that I look up for inspiration.
These are the dead writers that speak to me.

My professor explained and argued that I should read Latin American Writers, such as Pablo Neruda, Octavio Paz, Cesar Vallejo and many other great Latin American poets. "In order to know about your past and your heritage, " my professor claimed.

My professor's comments and concerns surprised me because I knew nothing else besides these western, canonized writers. At the time, I lived in a vacuum. I lived and breathed the best works from the English renaissance such as *The Tragic History of the Life and Death of Dr. Faustus* by Christopher Marlowe. I guess I was really "institutionalized" because by that time I only read the work of English writers just like any other traditional English major would have done. I spent so much time reading Chaucer, Milton, and Wordsworth that their words meant a whole world. I was driven only to learn from the best.

For a long time and even now, I wonder what my professor meant by "past" and "heritage." Didn't my professor know I am a Native of America? Did my professor mean my Mayan heritage? Was my professor talking about my Mexican past? Did my professor know that I had a Spanish heritage? Didn't my professor know my grandmother was a mulatto? Didn't my professor see my brown skin resembles a thousand Latino men, yet my brain and heart are unique … that I am what I am? Did my professor know I was an Undocumented Poet trying to write poetry in the United States?

I began to wonder what is my "past" and "heritage." Were these two words as dead as the dead writers who speak to me? I felt the need and the urge to hear my "past" and "heritage" speak to me, but for a long time, these words didn't mean a thing to me.

I have always wanted to state that my "heritage" and "past" are as tangled and knotted as a fisherman's nets in a dark, stormy night. For this reason, I have always dealt with misconceptions and stereotypes while learning poetry in graduate school. I always had a tough time trying to understand and to find an answer to my professor's words.

My professor believed the work of these Latino Poets and writers could make me more sympathetic towards topics such as politics and social conflicts that warp South America. I am sympathetic to these issues because my father, a campesino, lost his livelihood, his land, when one of the great financial depressions hit Mexico in the 90's. I have lived and survived this financial depression. I am what I am.

Moreover, throughout my whole graduate experience, I was mislabeled and misunderstood as a Latino Writer. Even one of my classmates had suggested that people like "me" should write about different topics and experiences. I wondered what my classmate meant by people like "me" and to what experiences this person was referring? Did my classmate mean the immigrant experience? Did my classmate mean an Undocumented person like me? Once again, I wanted to know if this person meant me, a man writing poetry in the United States, or everything else my classmate thought the color of my skin stands for? I didn't waste time with these useless comments. No, comments like this only pushed me to learn more about English Literature.

I lived alienated and unwilling to express my love and respect for the western, canonized writers. I ventured to write sestinas, villanelles, and sonnets only to hide them away because my classmates didn't have an interest on such dead and outdated forms. Yet, I am convinced that these forms are the vital foundation for any poet's work. As a result, this moment of alienation forced me to listen closely to the dead writers. They spoke to me clearly. I understood the need to read the classics such as *The Aeneid, Othello, Macbeth*, and many more. Institutionalized or not, the dead writers had had a great influence on my poetry and the man I am.

I was reluctant to read these Latino writers because at the time, their work didn't speak to my inner soul. I wasn't mature enough to understand their poetics. Feeling disconnected and alienated by the Latino writers, I returned to my western, canonized writers with such dedication and devotion. Shakespeare's *The Tempest* was of great comfort in those days. As a young man, I always wanted to read Shakespeare because I understood that any English major must understand his work in order to appreciate the beauty of English Literature. Shakespeare's usage of universal motifs such as death and life, love and war snared me to keep on learning about his work.

I grew up amazed reading and repeating alone Caliban's words,

> You taught me language; and my profit on't
> Is, I know how to curse. The red plague rid you
> For learning me your language.
> (I. 2. 437–39)

I related to Caliban's anger and frustration because just like Caliban I had been forced to learn a new language. I was forced to forget my native Mayan language and forced to learn Spanish, and just like Caliban, I lived in an alienated world listening to the voice of my dead.

Once, I was invited to read at a San Francisco bookstore, when a person from the audience asked me, "What are you reading nowadays in order to write poetry?" I felt eager and happy to share with the audience about this great writer, Ted Hughes, but once I said his name, I was shocked no one acknowledged such a great English writer. Since then, the words of my professor come back to haunt me; "You're stacked in the past, where only the dead writers dwell." This was a great moment of discouragement for me as a writer because I felt lonely in a world of the dead. However, I kept on reading Hughes' *Crow: From the Life and Songs of the Crow* with such ferocity that many of my published poems were influenced by this dark figure called the Crow. Once again, the dead spoke to me, and even now, writing these lines, I can hear the dead speaking to me.

In addition, another professor congratulated me for being in his poetry class whenever any Latino poet's work was studied. This professor looked up to me thinking that as a Hispanic male, I had better insights about these Latino writers than any one else in the class. What a great mistake.

Furthermore, I recalled another professor, who advised me to enroll in a Latin American class to study Pablo Neruda as my first graduate class. I didn't follow this professor's advice, and as a form of rebellion and to prove I could do well in any other class, I enrolled in ENG 853 Shakespeare Plays.

Once again, Shakespeare motivated me to explore themes such as life and death and our role as characters in this world. I did pretty well in the class as I learned from one of the great professors who never questioned my "heritage" or "past" and accepted my comments always with a scholar's objective point of view. I spent so much time talking with my professor about Shakespeare that every time I walked out my professor's office, I felt an indescribable feeling of acceptance and gratitude. For once, I felt someone understood me. My professor loved Shakespeare just like me. My English professor understood that Shakespeare is universal and anyone can read and comment about his work no matter where you come from, or what color of your skin is.

*

Many of my professors didn't understand that as an Undocumented, Immigrant Poet I had chosen to read and to be influenced by these western, canonized, male writers. They didn't understand that these dead writers speak to me in a loud and clear manner. They didn't understand that it doesn't matter who you are, there are some writers who speak to you louder than others. It doesn't really matter where you grew up, or who has influenced you, or in what country you have lived or grew up, or what language you speak, or the color of your skin ... Institutionalized or not; it is just like Walt Whitman wrote in his preface to *Leaves of Grass*, "The proof of a poet is that his country absorbs him as affectionately as he has absorbed it." This is the beauty of listening to the dead writers. They foresaw the future wisely. I chose to be the man that I am. I choose to be an American Poet.

One-Off

José Antonio Rodríguez

The time's running out and the list I and the couple of participants have put together on the chalkboard of the different roles/subjectivities we inhabit in our everyday lives reads like the self parsing itself out: student, friend, son/daughter, male/female/intersexed, romantic other, citizen/alien, gay/straight ... No one in this room inhabits all these roles but each of us certainly inhabits many, I say, hoping we can take a moment to appreciate the vast complexity of our lives. And I wonder about the cultural particularities of life here in a working-class wing of the city of Atlanta, of visiting this university in which I conduct a poetry workshop.

Hoping to reign in their focus and attention, I ask them to take a few minutes to jot down three roles they feel are particularly significant for them or hold special meaning. What roles do they most fear, do they most treasure, do they most fully inhabit? They scribble on their spiral notebooks. My eyes rest on the worn down desks, the flesh-colored plaster walls, and I am comforted by the absence of modern technology inside this classroom. Here, today, it is a relief.

We share some of the roles we've jotted down. I share mine in no specific order: immigrant, son, student. Now, I say, take a few minutes to recall an experience that challenged, dismantled, or revealed one of these subjectivities.

143

The plan was to have them write a poem that began at one moment in this experience, offering the participants a strong starting point that could prove generative and inspiring. A starting point that might serve to illustrate the important truth that our lives can be the stuff of poetry too—because after several years of living creative writing in the classroom, I've heard too many students who don't yet believe it—but I've run out of time. As a relatively young writer, I'm not always successful in framing these one-off workshops within the allotted time, and this irks me. In any case, I tell them as much and offer them this prompt as homework. At this precise moment I am reminded of a workshop lead by Mark Doty that I attended a few years ago, where he also gave us homework, and it tickles me. I don't feel so bad then, assigning homework.

As I'm wrapping up, puzzled briefly by the chalk on my hands—chalk that always smells of elementary school—one of the participants, a high school student, raises her hand.

"But what poets do we read?" she asks.

Having stressed earlier the importance of reading to the development of a writer, I sense only now the overwhelming implications of that statement, the enormity and amorphousness of the endeavor. I'm stuck. What DOES she read? Who? In what order? Where? What has she already read? After a few uhh's, I tell her a good beginners' poetry craft book with plenty of sample poems to illustrate themes and exercises, such as *The Poet's Companion*, may be a good place to start. Then I trickle out a few contemporary poets whose work I admire and recommend: Terrance Hayes, Naomi Shihab Nye, Mark Doty, Joe Weil. Marie Howe, I think but don't say. But I draw a blank after that brief list. If you enjoy a poet's work, I tell her, go to the book's acknowledgements page to see what journals have published them and visit the journals' websites, try and get your hands on an issue. It's a start, I think. And before I know it, the workshop ends and I'm gone and sitting at the airport gate waiting for my flight out and back to south Texas.

Gloria Anzaldúa, I think, when I search for other poets I could have suggested. Then I realize that if I had to pick one poet to call my biggest influence, the one whose poetry I am most grateful to have come across, I would pick her.

Years ago I was a struggling master's student in the English department at The University of Texas-Pan American—stumbling, scrambling, scribbling erratic attempts at poetry, afraid to speak the thing directly because it eluded me and I eluded it. The course was Mexican-American Literature and the reading assignment was *Borderlands: La Frontera*, a truly hybrid text, a trailblazer in redefining genre—combination of cultural criticism, spiritual treatise, autobiography, ethnography, poetry. When I finished reading it, my first thought was, "Where has this been all my life?" Then I lamented the years lived without Anzaldúa's beautiful words.

Influence, as I have heard it expressed, is often calculated by style. Whose poetry has been instrumental to the ways you construct your poems? In my case, though, Anzaldúa's influence is most significantly measured in content, themes, subject matter, tone. She was the first poet I came across who wrote about the concrete things I knew and wrote them with a mixture of sorrow, anger, and joy. Don't get me wrong, it wasn't that I hadn't appreciated poetry before hers. I certainly enjoyed the imagery, rhythms, and cadences of Robert Frost, of Walt Whitman, of Emily Dickinson, but the worlds they created on the page never felt immediate and when they wrote "we", I never really felt included. This is often part of the minority experience when confronting literature of the American canon. It was some other "we" that they were invoking, *those* Americans whom

they referred to and whom they called their own, Americans whom
I couldn't help but see as white and wealthy and distant.

My home in the town of McAllen, an overwhelmingly brown
town located in a far corner of Texas, a far corner of the United
State entire, didn't feel like it belonged in poetry. After so much
reading of snow in poetry and prose, it never occurs to you that
literature could be set anywhere that doesn't snow, ever, like south
Texas. But Anzaldúa wrote about arid lands, about nopales, about
the sweltering heat of migrant fieldwork, about cabbage crops, about
brown-eyed anguish and blue-eyed power. And she wrote about
the painfully magical place called the border—that bridge, that
river—la frontera, where belonging and unbelonging was always
being negotiated. Is always being negotiated. She said it: I may be
everything the center calls me, the embodiment of the margins,
but I will claim this space as my own and from it carve a new consciousness pregnant with conflict, beauty, silence, and song. As an
immigrant poet, as a brown poet, as a Spanish-speaking poet, as
a poor poet, as a queer poet, I felt found by her words. My poems
flowed then. The vast majority of them poorly crafted, much too
literal, not enough compression of meaning, but they were the best
beginning, nonetheless—a beginning of release, of permission, of
voice. The good stuff would come later. The best stuff, I'm thrilled to
know, is still ahead of me. But there she was at the beginning. Simply
put, she gave me license.

As the plane returning me home accelerates on the runway, the
weight of the mechanism bearing down the second before it leaves
the ground, I know if I had to pick an identity or subjectivity and
an experience that revealed it, the poem would be about becoming
a writer that day when I finished reading Anzaldúa's book. That day
would be the moment.

The airplane levels off, I take out my journal, I see the students at their desks, their inquisitive eyes, their eager pens, and I hope that they find the moments, or rather that the moments—the ones that destroy and create, that support and redefine, that challenge and reveal—find their way to words.

Travels through the Dark
William Stafford's Influence on a Nigerian Émigré Poet
Abayomi Animashaun

I'll begin by making clear that even though I have been an immigrant in America for nearly twenty years, I situate my work within the poetic traditions of the most populous country on the African continent. Thus, I am a Nigerian poet. But, just because I see myself as a Nigerian poet does not mean all the voices that inform my work are Nigerian.

*

To be sure, I chose to pursue poetry after attending a Derek Walcott reading. But, it was after reading William Stafford's collections of prose, *Crossing Unmarked Snow, Writing the Australian Crawl,* and *You Must Revise Your Life,* that I slowly, truly, began to work my way through the expansive landscape known as poetry.

Of the prose collections mentioned above (I would read *Down in My Heart* a few years later), I stumbled upon *Crossing Unmarked Snow* first. And, his statements on poetry in the book confirmed what I, at the time, felt:

"No matter who claims them, all good poems, the kind that are organically grown, are anonymous."

"The first thing you think of is really worth writing down. And the second. And the third..."

"We do not 'correct' a piece of writing; we question a life."

"...anyone can make writing a way of life, a practice that can lead to self-realization, to a fuller involvement in one's own experience."

*

Reading such statements as those above made me, someone who was just starting out, feel welcome. Intuitively, I didn't feel I was being pushed out and having the gates of poetry shut in my face because I was new to it. I knew I had deficiencies and a long reading list. But, reading this particular collection of prose made me feel there was a place for me in the room. In fact, it was after reading this collection that I permitted myself to be "reckless." To play soccer without a ball, or tennis without a net.

*

Playing Tennis with the Net Down

"...Writing poetry without form is like
playing tennis without a net."
　　　　—Robert Frost

I play tennis with the net down,
Rolled across the lawn and pushed

To the side, with sweat heavy on my chest
And the sun glaring on my back.

I practice a slow-paced serve that hangs
In the air long enough for me to travel
To the other side, bring the racquet low
And place another lob high.

All these years friends have pointed
And jeered. *This is no game,* they say.
What purpose to all this?
What point to prove?

Sometimes I watch them go at it.
The tightness on their faces,
The rules waiting to be bent,
All call me back to my ways.

Now children come and watch
The man who plays tennis with his shadow,
They ask if they can stretch the net
Across the lawn,

If they can play fishermen
In long boats on the waters
Ready for a big catch. I nod across at them:
'In this type of tennis, even fishing is possible.'

*

This conversation with Stafford, however, did not end with my first
attempts at the poem that would eventually become "Playing Tennis
with the Net Down." Through Stafford, I came to realize that some of

my ideas on writing were premature. For instance, I always thought poets and writers were people who had "something" to say. They had the really big ideas and all they had to do was sit down for hours to find the words to capture their big ideas. Stafford, helped me put that notion to rest with the first words of *Writing the Australian Crawl*:

> "A writer is not so much someone who has something to say as he is someone who has found a process that will bring about new things he would not have thought if he had not started to say them…"

I was hooked! And this was just the first sentence!! This was contrary to all I had heard and been taught. What seems so commonplace today—writing as a tool for thinking; writing as avenue toward insight and discovery—was, to me, completely revolutionary!

I had to give it a try. At first it was hard. Being receptive "to the first available news", and moving by feeling toward a thing, a village, or a country beyond me required a posture of mind that I wasn't used to. But, through a relinquishing of the little I knew, it became easier for me to "travel through the dark", with faith, abandon, and a willingness to remain lost.

*

In *You Must Revise Your Life*, Stafford talks, among other things, about his time as a conscientious objector to the Second World War (I would learn a good deal more about this in *Down in My Heart*) and how mornings to him were essential to his writing of poetry:

> "Because we had to work hard in the camps … we would be too tired for reading, writing, and study late in the evening. So some of us formed a group … for early morning literary activity. We would quietly get up at four A.M. or so and make

our way to the gathering place, where we could read and write till breakfast call."

This daily act of getting up before dawn to work was one Stafford practiced throughout his life. And, it was after reading this particular essay in this prose collection that I understood I didn't have to wait for inspiration to work. But, more precisely, I also came to understand that poetry required discipline. Not brick and mortar discipline! But, the kind of flexible discipline that allows one to enter comfortably and feel at home in the unknown. So, I too began the daily practice of waking up before dawn, traveling through the dark, and engaging whatever came my way.

*

4 A.M.

Even in the other Nigeria,
Where few are bound,

And the sun,
When it desires,
Dims its own light,

Even here,
Many get up at this hour
To engage in their own ritual—

The muezzin
Calls apples to prayers,

Imams remove their beards,
Paint their faces white,

And sit in long rows
Outside mosques for hours

Till from their silences
A parade of zebras emerge.

Slowly at first,
In ones.

Then in twos,
Resolved.

Followed by mimes,
Doing cartwheels,

Mangos throwing confetti,
Guavas juggling hats,

And elephants,
Pink and small as ants,

Hauling, with their trunks,
The first hours of dawn.

*

Among other things, "4 A.M.", is also a portrait of this Nigerian émigré poet early in the morning, when everyone is asleep. This poet has no agenda. Nor does this poet know where he'll end up.

This posture of mind, this steady, quiet, approach to poetry, was sown by William Stafford. Of course, his poems were also influential. But, for me, it was more his prose.

There would eventually be other writers: Fagunwa, Achebe, Soyinka. Elytis, Cavafy, Rilke. Machado, Jimenez, Gibran. And so many others.

But, it was through the old man from Hutchinson, Kansas that much about poetry, for me, became demystified. He opened the door and saved me years of needless toil.

Osip Mandelstam, A Lyric Voice

Ilya Kaminsky

> When a great singer sings, the skin of space and of time go
> taut, there is no corner left of silence or of innocence, the gown
> of life is turned inside out, the singer becomes earth and sky,
> time past and time to come are singing one of the songs of a
> single life.
>
> —John Berger[1]

> And if the song's in search of earth, and if the song's
> Ensouled, then everything vanishes
> To void, and the stars by which it's known,
> And the voice that lets it all be and be gone.
>
> —Osip Mandelstam

"I have no manuscripts, no notebooks, no archives," wrote Osip
Mandelstam, "I have no handwriting because I never write. I alone
in Russia work from the voice, while all around the wolf-bitch of
pack writers. What the hell kind of writer am I!? Get out, you fools!"[2]

To introduce this voice, one must first ask what is a lyric poet, and
what is a lyric impulse. A lyric poet is a self-professed "instrument"
of language who changes that language. And a lyric impulse? Here
is Marina Tsvetaeva, a contemporary of Mandelstam's:

> My difficulty (in writing poems—and perhaps other people's
> difficulty in understanding them) is in the impossibility of my

goal, for example, to use words to express a moan: nnh—nnh—
nnh. To express a sound using words, using meanings. So that
the only thing left in the ears would be nnh-nnh-nnh.[3]

*

January 3rd, 1891, Warsaw. To Emil and Flora Mandelstam, a boy
is born.

My father had absolutely no language; his speech was tongue-
tie and languagelessness. The Russian speech of a Polish Jew?
No. The speech of a German Jew? No again. Perhaps a special
Kurland accent? I never heard such ... speech ... where normal
words are intertwined with ancient philosophical terms of
Herder, Leibnitz, and Spinoza, the capricious syntax of a
talmudist, the artificial not always finished sentence: it was
anything in the world, but not a language, neither Russian nor
German.[4]

*The impossibility of my goal, for example, to use words to express
a moan: nnh—nnh—nnh. To express a sound using words, using
meanings.*

*

When as a boy Osip Mandelstam brought his poems to a venerable
journal of that time, the editor observed:

Mandelstam did not feel the Russian language as his own;
he observed it lovingly as if from a distance, finding its
beauty ... listening into it, flaming from mysterious victories over
it ... The Russian language itself was beginning to sound anew.[5]

I bring these testimonies not because they have to do with Mandelstam's father—and, to some extent, with the poet himself—being a

non-native speaker of the Russian language. I bring them because I believe that no great lyric poet ever speaks in the so-called "proper" language of his or her time. Emily Dickinson didn't write in "proper" English grammar but in *slant* music of fragmentary perception. Half a world and half a century away, Cesar Vallejo placed three dots in the middle of the line, as if language itself were not enough, as if the poet's voice needed to leap from one image to another, to make—to use Eliot's phrase—a raid on the inarticulate. Paul Celan wrote to his wife from Germany, where he briefly visited from his voluntary exile in France: "The language with which I make my poems has nothing to do with one spoken here, or anywhere."

*

But how to show this *privacy* of Mandelstam's Russian language while we discuss him in English? What is an English equivalent for *this*: "Voronezh; / Uronish ty menya il' provoronish, / Ne veronish menya ili vernesh, / Voronezh—blazh, Voronezh—voron, nosh." Reading these aloud, we cannot help but recall Gerard Manley Hopkins. The comparison with Hopkins also brings to mind Louise Bogan's claim that "many effects in Hopkins which we think of as triumphs of 'modern' compression are actually models of Greek compression, as transformed into English verse." Substitute "Russian" for "English," and she comes close to describing Mandelstam. Here is what Mandelstam's Greek instructor remembers:

> He would be monstrously late for our lessons and completely shaken by the secrets of Greek grammar that had been revealed to him. He would wave his hands, run about the room and declaim the declensions and conjugations in a sing-song voice. The reading of Homer was transformed into a fabulous event; adverbs, enclitics, and pronouns hounded

him in his sleep, and he entered into enigmatic personal
relationships with them ... He arrived at the next day with a
guilty smile and said, "I haven't prepared anything, but I've
written a poem." And without taking off his overcoat, he
began to recite ... He transformed grammar into poetry and
declared that the more incomprehensible Homer was, the more
beautiful ... Mandelstam did not learn Greek, he intuited it."[6]

He *intuited* it. From the inarticulate comes the new harmony. The
lyric poet wakes up the language; the speech is revealed to us in a
new, unexpected syntax, in music, in ways of organizing the silences
in the mouth. "You have no idea what kind of trash poetry comes
from," Anna Akhmatova wrote of her own process. From the very
beginning of his literary life, the readers of Mandelstam saw his
ability to remake the Russian language. They said he saw Russia
with a stranger's eyes. They said he wrote of an "imagined Russia."[7]
They said, sometimes disparagingly, that he was lost in his "own
language, his own *Russian Latin*."[8] But you could say this about any
great lyric poet.

*

A few years after Osip's birth, in 1897, the Mandelstams move to St.
Petersburg, where Osip's mother, Flora Osipovna, has "an almost
manic need"[9] for relocating from one apartment to another. One
wonders how this movement affected the poet, who later traveled
all over the Soviet Union, as if possessed, from Moscow to Kiev
to Armenia to the Crimea, looking for a home, an apartment, a
room—and yet when the apartment was finally granted to him, later
in life, no peace came:

I have lost my way in the sky—now, where?

*

Mandelstam's life is full of dualities, arguments, contradictions. A Jew born in Poland, he was Russian poetry's central figure in the twentieth century. A Modernist, he openly defended strict classical forms. He wrote in rich, formal verse structures. Then sometimes he didn't. He rarely titled his poems. Sometimes he did. He kept more than one version of the same lyric, and sometimes inserted the same stanza into different poems. He composed aloud and recited to his wife, who wrote the poems down. Mandelstam was Russia's "most civilized poet," "a child of Europe,"[10] yet he found his "fullest breath"[11] not in worldly European capitals but in exile in provincial town of Voronezh.

Perhaps such duality and contradiction, too, lie at the heart of a modern poet's lyric impulse, which brings together the rawest opposites to produce that "divine harmony." But what *is* a lyric impulse in a time of war and revolution? Is it an individual voice? Could this voice speak for the nation? Can one person's voice speak of the epic events of his time? Can, indeed, those events be channeled through the lyric voice?

*

In all this ocean of new rooms and suitcases, perhaps the only island was a bookshelf:

> The bookcase of early childhood is a person's lifetime companion. The disposition of its shelves, the selection of books, the color of the spines is perceived as the color, height, disposition of world literature itself.[12]

Or perhaps the island is the city itself. St. Petersburg, Petrograd, Piter, Leningrad—this "brother, Petropolis," the dying city, the city as a ship, the Flying Dutchman, around which his mother moves her

furniture from one building to another, a city where he is brought as
a Jew, the capital of the vast Slav empire, here he writes his poetry,
later to be called "Petersburgian," though he has defined the city as
much as it him:

> You, with square windows,
> Squat houses in rows,
> Hello gentle,
> Hello winter,
> Petersburg, Petersburg,
> A thousand hellos.

*

What year is it? 1911. Mandelstam publishes his first poem. In St.
Petersburg a group of young poets form "The Guild of Poets," nam-
ing themselves "craftsmen of the word." Nikolai Gumilyov is the
"Master" of this guild. His wife, Anna Akhmatova, is "secretary."
Mandelstam becomes the Guild's "first violin."[13]

They call Shakespeare, Villon, and Rabelais their mentors, sug-
gesting that Western European, not Russian, culture is their north
star. As time will show, little unites their poetry except for a shared
aim at precision. Mandelstam:

> Everything has become heavier and more massive; thus man
> must become harder, for he must be the hardest thing on earth;
> he must be to the earth what the diamond is to glass.

In 1912 they call themselves Acmeists.

*

Like St. Petersburg itself, Acmeism is a longing for clarity of
architecture, is a jump from darkness (of national poverty, of igno-
rance) that surrounds it, is—as Mandelstam famously said—"a nos-

talgia for world culture." Their opponents? The Symbolists. Yes, it is
the old question of fathers and sons—Gippus, a leading Symbolist
poet, was Mandelstam's grade school teacher. Symbolists believed
that the visible here-and-now was illusory and that everything is in
any case fated to shatter or decompose—a prospect that filled them
with fearful presentiment. In this world of visions, the language is
blurred. Opposed to this, Acmeists demand "classical" precision of
language, formal elegance:

> One often hears: "That's fine and good, but it's yesterday." But
> I say: Yesterday has not yet been born. In reality, it hasn't even
> taken place yet. I want Ovid, Pushkin and Catullus all over
> again—I am not satisfied with the historical Ovid, Pushkin and
> Catullus.[14]

Mandelstam's first book—called *Stone*—appears in 1913. He is 23.
The Great War is about to begin. In three years he will meet Marina
Tsvetaeva. In four years the Russian empire will fall.

*

And, what happens around this little bubble in St. Petersburg, this
little café where young poets meet, the Stray Dog? In Russia, Chagall
is emerging as a painter, Rachmaninov and Stravinsky are changing
music, Stanislavski and Meyerhold are revolutionizing theater, Diaghi-
lev is changing the classical Russian ballet.

And, abroad, in France, Apollinaire, inspired by Whitman, is
leading the same revolt against the French Symbolists. Pound is
swashbuckling through the tradition, taking what he wants and
throwing out what he doesn't.

*

Yet, a comparison with Pound or Apollinaire is misleading. Both
French and American bards come on the heels of *centuries* of poetic

tradition. Mandelstam and his generation are the poets of the Silver age of Russian literature. Pushkin, the father of the Russian poetic tradition, was the Golden Age[15] And Pushkin died only a few decades before them.

And what was before Pushkin?

Darkness.

*

Pushkin:

> Russia long remained alien to Europe. Accepting the light
> of Christianity from Byzantium she participated in neither
> the political upheavals nor the intellectual activity of the
> Roman Catholic world. The great epoch of Renaissance had
> no influence on her ... [Enslaved by Tatars] for two dark
> centuries only clergy preserved the pale sparks of Byzantine
> learning ... But the inner life of the enslaved people did not
> develop. The Tatars did not resemble the Moors. Having
> conquered Russia they did not give it algebra nor Aristotle.[16]

Russia had no history, said Chaadaev, the nineteenth-century public intellectual who left Russia and was either brave (or crazy) enough to return. But when Chaadaev declared this, he had overlooked language. Russia had no history and no literature, but it had its language. And soon enough Chaadaev's contemporaries, Pushkin and Gogol among them, began to develop one of Europe's youngest— and fieriest—literary traditions.

*

This astonishing youth of the Russian poetic tradition is the true reason for Mandelstam's generation's "nostalgia for world culture." While Westerners such as Pound were looking elsewhere to *remake* the poetry of their time, the Russians, surrounded by the darkness of centuries devoid of literature, looked to classics of other languages to *create* their country's poetic line. Tolstoy and Dostoevsky were able to write epics as late as the last half of the nineteenth century because there were no great epics in the language before them. Creating classics was a modern project for the Russians: it had the urgency of the time. Mandelstam:

> Classical poetry is perceived as *that which ought to be*, not that which has already been ... Contemporary poetry ... is naïve. ... Classical poetry is the poetry of revolution."[17]

*

1917. At the height of the Revolution Mandelstam, without much money,

> having by some miracle got a room in the Astoria [*the* most elegant hotel in St. Petersburg], took a tub bath several times each day, drank the milk that had been left at his door by mistake, and lunched at the Donon, where the proprietor, out of his mind, extended credit to everyone.[18]

What is an image of a lyric poet in the days of the Revolution? A young man taking baths several times each day and drinking milk while bombs explode outside his hotel room?

*

In a few months his best friend, the poet Nikolai Gumilyov, will be shot. Mandelstam will run from city to city for several years during the Civil War that follows the Revolution. He is imprisoned many times: Reds think that he (an intellectual) is a spy sent by the White Army; Whites think that he (a Jew) is one of the Communists.

In those days, "Mandelstam was always ardent and always hungry, but as everyone was hungry at the time, I should have said even hungrier than other people. Once he called on us wearing a raincoat and nothing else."[19]

*

1919. Kiev. He marries Nadezhda. From this date until 1938 they are never apart. For years he and his new wife will walk through the ruins of an empire, like a modern Don Quixote and Sancho Panza. What are facts?

After the Revolution he applies to Gorky (through the Union of Poets) for a sweater and a pair of trousers; Gorky refused the trousers.[20]

*

Antonio Machado suggested: "In order to write poetry, you must first invent a poet who will write it." Whether Mandelstam was inventing himself, or being forged by the pressure of his times, one thing is obvious: some of the best writing comes in his darkest personal hours: hunger in Crimea, the restless life in Moscow, exile in Voronezh. "Restlessness was the first sign," Nadzhda wrote,

> that he was working on something and the second was the moving of his lips ... His head was twisted around so that his chin almost touched his shoulder; he was twirling his walking stick with one hand and resting the other on one of the stone steps to keep his balance ... When he was composing" he always hand a great need of movement. He either paced the room or kept going outside to walk the streets.[21]

And his view of the poetic vocation? Perhaps not surprisingly, it is rather close to that of his contemporary, W.H. Auden:

Whatever its actual content and over interest, every poem is rooted in imaginative awe. Poetry can do a hundred and one things, delight, sadden, disturb, amuse, instruct—it may express every possible shade of emotion, and describe every conceivable kind of event, but there is only one thing that all poetry must do; it must praise all it can for being and for happening.[22]

*

What is around him? The Russian Empire is now the land of Five Year Plans, with political purges, kholkhozes, starvation in the Ukraine (where he and Nadezhda were married). He is working at a journal, he writes children's books, he translates. He is falsely accused of stealing another's translation, and there follows an ugly public trial. He slaps the face of Alexei Tolstoy, *the red count*, the venerable novelist of that day. A scandal.

He asks the secretary at Litfond (a financial foundation for supporting Soviet writers) about the costs of a coffin. Why? He doesn't want a coffin of his own; when he dies they can bury him without one. A scandal. He wants to be paid for his death up front.

*

Why repeat these anecdotes? *I live for two things in life* (said Akhmatova): *gossip and metaphysics.*

*

We tell these stories because we want an answer to the question: what is the lyric poet's response to the epic events of his time? Here is Mandelstam's friend, Ilya Ehrenburg: "Poets greeted the Russian Revolution with wild shouts, hysterical tears, laments, enthusiastic frenzy, curses." Mandelstam "alone understood the pathos of the events, comprehended the scale of what was occurring." Brodsky: "[Mandelstam's was] perhaps the only sober response to the events which shook the world ... His sense of measure and his irony were enough to acknowledge the epic quality of the whole undertaking."

Is this the same man who was drinking milk in the bath of the expensive hotel while around him the city exploded? We can't resolve his contradictions, but perhaps noting them can give us one way to speak about his lyric impulse.

*

Most 20th century Russian readers would argue that the poet, any poet, *does* have a moral responsibility to his people. In that country, as a saying goes, a poet is a great deal more than just a poet. In pre-fifth-century Greece, "the poet was still the undisputed leader of his people ... The Greeks always felt that a poet was in the broadest and deepest sense the educator of his people"[23] Many a Russian poet shared this feeling during the first twenty years of the twentieth century.

But what does it mean to speak for one's people? And, just who *are* one's people?

*

When the government demands poems about collective farms, he writes about Greek myths. Later, when they demand patriotic songs for the working class, he writes an ode to "my necrotic, psychotic age." "I want to spit in the face of every writer who first obtains permission and then writes," he says. "I want to beat such writers over the head with a stick ... placing a glass of police tea before each one."

And thereby speaks for his people. In one single human's voice. In a tone that is direct enough, playful enough, to be understood by his people's ears.

He wrote:

> An heroic era has opened in the life of the word. The word is flesh and bread. It shares the fate of bread and flesh: suffering. People are hungry. The state is even hungrier. But there is something hungrier yet: time.

Such is a lyric poet's relationship to his time. He is both inside and outside of it; he suffers its immediate circumstances in the context of centuries. *The noise of time*—the title of his prose memoir—can also be translated as the hum of time, and humming was a part of this poet's writing process—almost as if the very substance of time were transformed within him, by means of him. "For an artist," Mandelstam wrote, "a worldview is a tool or a means, like a hammer in the hands of a mason, and the only reality is the work of art itself."

*

While Akhmatova, in her *Requiem*, wrote what is probably the only lasting epic cycle of that time, Mandelstam offers us something entirely different: a voice singing outside of the people, a voice laughing and cursing, praising, asking for a Reader! Adviser! Doctor! and waiting for the arrest, and jumping from the second story window out of desperation, and asking a friend in the street for cash. It isn't the voice of a country, it is the voice of one human, a voice so naked in its feeling and rich in its music that it could be spoken by anyone:

> *I have lost my way in the sky—now, where?*

*

Why speak of him in quotations. Why fragments? "Destroy your manuscript," he wrote, "but save whatever you have written in the margins."[24]

*

Scholars rarely speak about the radical changes in his poetics over the years. Beckett, they say, decided to write in French because his English was getting "too good," too poetic.

And Mandelstam? He begins as a shy Jewish boy writing in a voice of high culture with numerous references to Homer, Ovid, and ends, in 1930s with lyrics that often explore low styles, are able to be surreal and down-to-earth at the same time. It is as if Tennyson suddenly began to write in a style of Emily Dickinson.

*

Not long before this he reads his epigram to Stalin ("We Live") to a few friends, one of whom is the informer. What are facts? Exile. Where he jumps from that window. A new exile, Voronezh. Where he writes his best poems. Return.

> He was a "Holy Fool," a iurodivyi of seventeenth-century Russia, a "bird of God" (he loved swallows and identified himself with the goldfinch); he was one of those imitators of Christ, God's fools, who were during Russia's times of troubles alone privileged to criticize the State. Like Ovid, he was an exile dreaming of Rome; like Dante, he wrote poems to "the measure and rhythm of walking." All poets were exiles, "for to speak means to be forever on the road."[25]

Yet another exile: Death in the camp. Unmarked grave.

*

And poems? After his death his poems were memorized by his wife and a few friends. They didn't keep originals in a written form. They wrote poems from memory, burned the paper, wrote poems from memory, burned the paper, wrote poems from memory, burned the paper. This continued for some decades.

*

What are we to do with it, this voice, in another language? Here, listen, again, to these lines:

> Pusti menya, otdai menya, Voronezh;
> Uronish ty menya il' provoronish,
> Te veronish menya ili vernesh,
> Voronezh—blazh, Voronezh—voron, nosh.

*

And, again:

> Pusti menya, otdai menya, Voronezh;
> Uronish ty menya il' provoronish,
> Te veronish menya ili vernesh,
> Voronezh—blazh, Voronezh—voron, nosh.

You don't understand? He, too, once, heard a language he didn't speak:

> I experienced such joy in pronouncing sounds forbidden to Russian lips, mysterious sounds, outcast sounds, and perhaps, at some deeper level, even shameful sounds. There was some magnificent boiling water in a tin teapot, and suddenly a pinch of marvelous black tea was tossed into it. That's how I felt about the Armenian language.

And, another poet said: "The language with which I make my poems has nothing to do with one spoken here, or anywhere."

Another poet said: "my difficulty (in writing poems—and perhaps other people's difficulty in understanding them) is in the impossibility of my goal, for example, to use words to express a moan: nnh—nnh—nnh. To express a sound using words, using meanings. So that the only thing left in the ears would be nnh-nnh-nnh."

I have lost my way in the sky—now, where?

Notes

1. John Berger, *And Our Faces, My Heart, Brief as Photos.*
2. Mandelstam, *Fourth Prose.*
3. Marina Tsvetaeva, *"Writing books and notebooks,"* September 1940, tr. Jean Valentine and Ilya Kaminsky.
4. *Prose of Osip Mandelstam*, Brown tr, p. 90.
5. Sergei Makovskii, *Portraits of Contemporaries (Portrety Sovremenikov)*, New York, Chekhov Publishers, 1955, p. 377–398.
6. Konstantin Mochulsky, Vstrecha, 2, (1945), 30–1.
7. Vladimir Markov.
8. Brown, *Osip Mandelstam.*
9. Evgeny Mandelstam, *Vospominaniya*, p. 125.
10. George Ivask's statement.
11. Akhmatova's statement.
12. Mandelstam, *Noise of Time.*
13. Akhmatova's phrase.
14. Mandelstam, *Slovo I Kultura*, 203.
15. Three well known poets before Pushkin—Lomonosov, Trediakovsky and Derzhavin—are universally accepted as minor, compared to Pushkin. The beautiful, and very moving early epic, *Lay of Igor's Campaign*, is only

available in a 19th century copy; a number of scholars argue that it was actually written in the 19th century.

16. *Critical Prose of Alexander Pushkin*, edited and translated by Carl Proffer, Indiana University Press.

17. Mandelstam, *Slovo I Kultura*.

18. Artur Lourie, VP, III (1963).

19. Igor Stravinsky and Robert Craft, *Retrospectives and Conclusions* (New York, 1969), p. 237.

20. Nadezhda Mandelstam, *Hope Abandoned*, p. 63.

21. Nadezhda Mandelstam, *Hope Against Hope*, p. 186.

22. "Making, Knowing, and Judging," W.H. Auden.

23. Jager, *Paideia*, p. 35.

24. Brown, The Prose of Mandelstam, p. 187.

25. Sydney Monas, *Collected Poems of Osip Mandelstam*.

IV: The Émigré Poet in America

Christopher Columbus Was A Damn Blasted Liar

The Narrative of Discovery in Global Literature

Matthew Shenoda

Some years ago I sat amongst a group of people influential in the contemporary literary scene in the United States. As I listened to one of the individuals (who holds some significant decision-making power in the literary world) speak about a writer that they "discovered" and whose "career" they helped launch, I was struck by the way the narrative was unfolding. I sat curiously listening to this hubris, this Columbusesque narrative, trying to understand the fascination for the speaker to spin such a tale. It so happened the writer at the center of this conversation was no stranger to me, it was someone whom I knew quite well. As the story went on and others around the table congratulated this person for their stellar work in "discovering" this young writer, I couldn't shake the way this narrative negated significant parts of this writers' life and lived experiences.

Too often have I heard editors, grant makers, and educators talk about "discovering" this or that writer and too often has that writer been a person of color, often from a country outside of the United States. Is this act of "discovery" a real possibility or is it a hold over from a colonial mentality that shapes the way in which writers of color in particular are still shaped and understood in the present literary landscape?

At the core of this telling was not an act of malice or even a conscious sense of power and privilege. The individuals around the table clearly and earnestly appreciated this writer's contributions to the world, or should I say to *their* world. You see, as is often the case, this writer they spoke of, as all writers serious about their craft, labored for many years and worked intimately within various communities before they were "discovered." And where is the room for that reality? For even to say this person is "new" to this landscape is quite different than to claim "discovery," for newness implies a history, implies a trajectory, implies a mutual relationship as one who is new to a place is also new to the people of that place. But a narrative of discovery seems somehow to negate an individual's history and experiences. What's more is that this narrative is doubly damaging to the so called "immigrant writer." Much like Columbus' narrative of discovery, this kind of telling negates a person's indigenaity and community.

In US literary narratives, the "immigrant writer" is somehow only fully birthed once they arrive on US soil. There may be small recollections of their terrible pasts in their home country, but their real moment of virtue and dare I say, freedom, only happens once they are "discovered" in the United States. All this to say that the things they have written, taught, been taught, or cultivated in their home nations are largely negated. They are born anew in this land of plenty and as such are ripe for assimilation by those in power. Their contribution to the literary ethos of the United States seems ancillary to the fact that "we" have given them so much. There is in this power dynamic an uneasy sense of ownership and indebtedness. Rarely is it that those who control the literati of this nation recognize that *they* would in fact be lesser had it not been for those writers widening and helping re-imagine the ways we understand literature, and frankly, life in this country.

My goal here is to roughly sketch just some of the issues that arise when we engage this topic, in hopes that a conversation can ensue amongst my fellow writers and readers of contemporary literature. By no means are my comments here meant to be comprehensive or exhaustive, but rather a primer to think about how we have an obligation to continue to engage literature in the 21st century.

To begin with we must unpack what I will call the affliction of parochialism, a reality all too common in literary (especially poetry) circles. This affliction is defined foremost by an inability to see outside of one's self, one's own confines, geographies, institutions, regions, and nation. Because writers too often affiliate with other writers, to be struck by this affliction is easier than one might think. If we read the same books, journals, and magazines, frequent the same virtual, cultural, and institutional spaces, we significantly hinder our ability to accept a world that is much wider in breadth, taste, and significance than the one we inhabit. We talk too commonly of a global age, or global literatures, but few embody such a reality. Instead, we occasionally allow "others" entry into this world and rarely venture outside of it ourselves, and this is the fundamental problem.

Not only is this an issue for the writer in question, but also for the reader, editor, grant maker, educator, etc. This kind of narrative puts the responsibility of a global reality on those from "other" places and rarely implicates, challenges, or educates the largely white members of the literary power structure in the U.S. Rarely is the editor challenged to have to engage in the home communities of these writers they "discover." Rarely are they held accountable to understand the roots and antecedents of these writer's aesthetics and literary traditions. Rarely are they called to rethink, realign or question their own tastes, interpretations, and aesthetic leanings. This reality creates a sorely uneven "global literature" where one group is indeed global and the other an apprehensive tourist given the power to shape their literary tourism as they see fit, never forced to face a rainy day on their perfectly curated literary vacation; always orchestrating how the world we all live in will be defined.

The Guyanese reggae band Arkaingelle sings in one of their tracks a simple summation of this predicament: "justice for all, not just those in the United States." Once we abandon our nationalistic sense of literature and begin to question our own assumptions about literature, notions of taste, craft, and aesthetics only then will we begin to approach a true and equitable global literature.

Notes

The quote "Christopher Columbus was a damn blasted liar" comes from the Burning Spear track, "Columbus," first released on the album *Hail H.I.M.* (EMI, 1980).

To Be A Poet in America
Shabnam Piryaei

It's like being a superhero. Or, more specifically, like being an amnesia-ridden superhero—utterly forgetting, living and behaving normally, then, suddenly, crossing a threshold and glimpsing this superhuman, miraculous *power*. That *you* have. And then perhaps being terrified or giddily ignited by the sheer scope of it. The spiritual depth of it. And the immense responsibility to *keep going*. I don't know how else to describe it. This is what it means for me, at the best, most disciplined and focused times, to be a poet—in general.

Poetry has always been embedded in my life; and to some degree this omnipresence of poetry is intrinsic to Iranian culture. For an enormously large number of Iranians, poetry isn't peripheral or abstract to their daily lives. It's present in the most intimate, quotidian, spiritual, traditional, and popular aspects of Iranian life. And it succeeds in achieving this without compromising the poetry itself, without reducing the potency or the quality of the literature in an effort to make it more accessible. Iranians in Iran memorize entire poems that they carry with them throughout their lives. They buy poem-stanzas on street corners along with packets of gum. Every Nowrooz, to mark and celebrate the new year, broadcasters on Iranian television and radio networks read poems aloud to their audi-

ences. Can you imagine an NBC or Fox News correspondent opening a book by William Shakespeare or Langston Hughes to read a
poem after the ball drops in New York City?

I have long lamented the peripheral position of poetry, particularly non-performative poetry, in American culture; and not just
this, but the general American population's *aversion* to it. In a TED
talk, while making a point about "getting poetry off the shelves and
more into public life", the poet Billy Collins said, "When you get a
poem on a billboard, or on the radio, or on a cereal box ... it happens
to you so suddenly that you don't have time to deploy your anti-
poetry deflector-shields that were installed in high school." I am a
proponent of bringing poetry more into the public sphere. It has
been a common practice for me throughout my work; whether I'm
producing fiction, drama or film, I always make a point to include
poetry. I suppose this combining of genres is, in part, an advertise-
ment for poetry, a broadening of its audience, a way to trick people
into experiencing it, into getting them more familiar with it in order
to evade and/or soften their "anti-poetry deflector-shields." Here in
the U.S., there is an acute discomfort with the abstractness of poetry,
with the work involved for the reader, and a sense of "otherness" that
in many cases is a product of the way poetry is frequently taught in
schools. Readers tend to want *answers*. They want to know *what it all
means*. There is something about the ambiguity, or more precisely,
the multi-meaning-ed quality of poems that can unsettle and frus-
trate readers. It's hard for many readers to accept that, sure, maybe
the author herself was musing on the experience of war, but if the
poem is resonating with you in a deep way in relation to the loss of
your mother to cancer, that doesn't make it any less right, or true, or
real of an interpretation. Good poetry, like all good art, reflects our
complexity, our ambiguity; this gesturing toward countless truths is

part of what makes art so very valuable. Demanding immediate and clear-cut answers of it reduces it, in the same way that demanding a person to be only one thing reduces and misrepresents them. The reaction to poetry, particularly poetry written for the page—that which a reader experiences quietly and in solitude—is mixed. My experience is that people tend to be exhausted with even the idea of having to read a poem and decipher its meaning only to be left ultimately confused by it. Admittedly, reading poetry *can* require work. But it's a delicious work, and—honestly "work" is not even accurate—it requires engagement, presence, listening. Even I, as a poet myself, sometimes sense my own reluctance when faced with the task of reading a poem. Because it demands a kind of stopping, a patience, a slowing down that clashes with and confuses my current internet-shaped thinking and processing pace (a problem I repeatedly face in my writing as well if I don't step away). But oh. My. God. Reading poetry can be a *divine* experience. Holy. I believe in poetry. I believe in its power as an art form and as a crucial method of expression. I believe in the jaw-dropping way it can pack revelations into a mere handful of carefully assembled words. I'm not arguing that poetry is a superior art form; it is art, and all the manifestations of art, all creative expression, when honest, coming from the heart, and true to the unique identity of the artist, are equally valuable. But poetry is *my* art form. It is how I most precisely speak. Creating it resonates with my spirit in a way that feels over and over like a fresh, undiscovered, and yet also deeply familiar, hallelujah.

To be a poet in America means to be an artist in the world, and part of a long literary tradition. To be an immigrant poet in America often mean publishers and readers want or expect your poetry to be specifically about your immigrant-ness, about your ethnic, cultural and historical identity. Being an Iranian woman in the world of art or journalism is a hot commodity right now, and has been for a while, particularly if the subject of your work is the plight of Iranian or Muslim women. For some artists and writers, these identity-related issues are precisely what they *need* to express; others, however, may be tempted to create work around these issues simply in order to appeal to or garner an audience. What this means is that sometimes a writer might feel their work will be better received if they speak about what it's like to be a woman driver in Tehran rather than their experiences at Burning Man or quotidian aspects of day-to-day American life. Sometimes this feeling of obligation is felt by the artist not because of external pressure, but because of a sense of personal and moral responsibility as an immigrant (or a Black woman, or a lesbian, or a Muslim … etc.) with a platform. And this curiosity on the part of publishers and readers isn't rootless. As an Iranian woman, I understand there appears to be a scarcity of "my voice", and this sparseness of visibly accessible information and perspective can lead to a curiosity on the part of non-Iranians about life in Iran, particularly the experiences of Iranian women. As an Iranian-American woman I am frequently subjected to a personal and political line of questioning that a white American would never have to face when meeting someone for the first time. Personally, I don't mind these kinds of exchanges (most of the time); they allow me to have a more honest interaction with strangers, rather than having to engage in small talk (which I don't like, and my dislike of which causes me to frequently pose jarring or seemingly out-of-place questions to cut through the fluff and arrive at a much more intimate, eye-to-eye space). But others aren't so comfortable with interrogations about their personal histories, and this is their right—no one should be coerced or cornered into being a representative of their people. But I only bring this up to say that I understand this curiosity can exist, both in day-to-day interactions and in works of art, because of a lack of knowing about the other. However, there are other reasons, non-curiosity reasons, for the wanting-you-to-write-about-your-identity; the same reasons that explain why, rather than being shelved in the general Fiction and Poetry aisles, or (gasp) in the Classics section, novels by Toni Morrison, essays by James Baldwin, plays by Suzan-Lori Parks, and poetry by June Jordan are frequently placed in the African-American Literature segment of bookstores, and brought to the foreground each February for a special table display. The danger comes when the identity of the writer, rather than enriching the reception of the work, leads to an external limitation, a peripheralizing from the "main" canon of literature.

As an Iranian-American poet, my being an American poet often gets lost in my Iranian-ness, in a way that I don't think would happen if I were born in Ireland and came to the U.S. when I was two. Truthfully, I don't feel that I'm only an American artist; my Iranian culture and heritage is an enormous part of my identity and worldview. However I don't need anyone to tell me that it *has* to be a part of my art, and I don't want it to be the *only* lens through which I, and my work, are viewed.

Ultimately, however, the position of poetry in current American culture, the pressure to address a distinct set of questions in one's work, and the possible relegation of one's work to non-mainstream shelves should play no part in the actual writing process, in the laboring and production of each individual poem; they are factors that can be faced and negotiated after the piece has been written. Because, simply, the work must be done, and it must be done candidly, creatively, and true to everything the writer is at the moment she is writing the poem. No matter what is going on outside, the poet must bring herself back to the poem, she must cross that threshold, and she must *keep going.*

An Émigré Poet in America

Marilène Phipps-Kettlewell

To be a poet is to hurt—I came, I saw, I hurt. We stand, we vouch, we lie—the truth we want is not—tis a dream we have of a life we knew in a world we lost. The cross we bear, we brought—America was brave and bold and here for us, who ventured forth with ills to tell. Love's conditions, we knew; methods of war, we learnt; the clothes we wear, we chose anew. Foreignness is a daily undressing and repairing of self. I am traveling through, not meant to stay. My poetry is but a lie, if only crafted words about a world I failed to join and laud. America is not at fault, if fault we seek. The culprit is my heart—inflexible yet soft, hushed yet shrill, intolerant yet raw. My skin is a hide, a window, an affliction not unique.

Other children lived inside themselves, safely by the fire in mussed sleep, while I went outside into new snow at dawn to see the field, dressed as a poet, before breakfast. Ah … the brightness of the sun! Ah … the pull of the wind in tall firs! And the crunchy shush of snow under my traveler's foot! There then, I felt I exist, and it is dear. But how can this be, when the only shushing underfoot I once cherished was the sound of sand on the beach of the island where I grew?

I turned to watch and linger over my old footsteps; but why? A mouse, dark brown and cold, ran out of one as if from a gulf it just escaped. He ran over the top of the snow, exposed, belly scraping the ice, persisting onward, yet only to fall and pass into another footstep ahead. I hope he got to where he was going, this modern mouse, watched over by a lone, modern Orpheus, a poet turning to see the cherished face she missed, and hurt, old steps recalled! Ah ... truly this country we crowd is not the fiend, is not the death—the poet's foe is but regret.

And God watched me repent, as He knew I would. Saint Francis now stands outside, birds pecking seeds at his stone feet. Death has undone the chains once clasped to my ancestors' limbs. Nowadays, they lean free on clouds to spy what gestures I may draw, what steps I carve on trails I pick. Cats and creatures left in my care have calmed the fear I feel. If they, so small, find love and help in one so vain as me, then I for sure would be seized by One manifold my size and worth, and though my face in His own likeness may be.

God my heaven, God my aim, God my help! A poet is your bard, or is nothing. America is not the world. The world is not my land. My land is not of this earth. This earth is not my home. I care not for the noise, the concrete, the cars, the grim towers of rock and glass that reflect others likewise grey, built to intimidate, but not house. I care not for the hustle, greed, and frauds of people growing in crowds wanting to vociferate, trample, defile, and masturbate for display, beings made puppets of fashion to serve the politics of the day.

To be a poet is to charm. To be a poet is to console. To be a poet is to silence. Sounds I listen for are those that tear, linger, and haunt. Resonance worth converting is that which enchants, dispels, and restores. As translator of echoes in the universe, the poet is a vibrating instrument, inherently unstable and crude. True poets kneel beside an ant bearing a load beyond its measure, are humbled each Spring by grace in an ungainly possum's purpose and gait, and

moved to see how goldfish surface throughout each day, to repeatedly grasp for the small second of time during which they may catch
a portion of the breath afforded by a world outside their natural element, one to them infinitely vast, but to which they are instinctually
drawn, for they know it to be essential and true.

On Being an Immigrant Poet in America

Barbara Jane Reyes

> "Imagine an entire culture that is passed down for thousands
> and thousands of years through the spoken word and
> narrative, so the whole of experience is put into narrative
> form—this is how the people know who they are as a people,
> and how individuals learn who they are."
> —Leslie Marmon Silko[1]

I immigrated to San Francisco in 1973; I was two years old. My parents had previously moved here, in 1969. They rented a small unit in an apartment building near Mitchell's Ice Cream in the Mission District, decades before the area became hip. My mother flew back to Manila in 1971 and gave birth to me. She returned to San Francisco, leaving me and my older sister in the care of our grandparents, aunts, and teenage uncle, who we thought was our older brother. My parents dove into the American grind, saved up, and two years later, my sister and I arrived here, into the arms of our parents, two people we did not know.

The story I've always been told is that back in Manila, and sensing our impending departure, I hid my uncle's car keys under my grandmother's spinster sister's bed, and that upon arriving in a dreary and rainy San Francisco, I cried for days and days. A trip to Disneyland did not assuage me. Other stories of that time entail me throwing up and ruining the interior of my mom's brand new Toyota Celica.

My parents, hardworking immigrants that they were, bought their first home a couple of years later. We moved to the suburbs, Fremont, to be exact, just north of Silicon Valley before it became widely known as Silicon Valley, and where we had a backyard, a cat, and a garden. My grandmother came from the Philippines, lived with us, and took care of us as both my parents worked. In the 1970s in Fremont, among my classmates' parents, my mom was one of the only moms who actually worked full time. My sisters and I attended private schools, took Honors English, Advanced Placement History, and Calculus. We scored high on the SATs, attended big (maybe even prestigious) universities. Decades later, we are paying mortgages and property taxes.

I tell you this story, not to brag, but to give you an idea of what I think was my parents' American Dream. And I am thinking about this American Dream, and American Dream as mythology, because I am thinking about being an "immigrant poet." Stories about my family and the English language, of my parents being apprehensive to speak English in public spaces, of me being tongue tied hence shy and bookish around my American classmates, all of these stories belong in the realm of mythology now.

And that's what's happened to my poetry. It's entered the realm of mythology.

My interest in writing about "the homeland," and "my culture," has not faded in my four decades of privileged American living, or in my two decades of writing and publishing in this country, or in my three years immersed in my MFA program, and not because of nostalgia or familial obligation.

My history, and my family history have always had documents and artifacts: posed and candid photographs, home movies, report cards, detention slips we forged with my parents' signatures, diplomas and degrees, marriage certificates, evidence of immunization, naturalization papers, Philippine and American passports, Facebook posts, and Instagram accounts.

My family history also has its share of lore and folklore. Oral tradition has ruled our self-knowledge, and with oral tradition has come multiple, sometimes quarreling, versions of "truth"; has come hearsay, from which all those wonderful stories that begin, "I wasn't there, but I heard that…"; has come this wonderful phenomenon called tsismis (chisme, gossip), in which everyone gets to speak, some with authority, some with the power of speculation, some only under the condition of anonymity.

This is the largely subjective, undocumented substance that interests me—the quarreling, multiple versions and interpretations of events, reliable and unreliable narrators, secret tellers, disavowers, eyewitnesses, fabricators, yarnspinners. Rather than dismiss any of these artful tellers, I think of how much they must know, what wisdom they contain and how much they withhold, either because nobody has ever asked, or because the message they have accepted and internalized is that their stories are not legitimate, that they are petty and superfluous, because their stories do not conform to the master narrative.

Oral tradition has made me suspicious of single, authoritative texts and master narratives. Instead, I am drawn to what persists and survives despite mainstream cultural insistence upon single, authoritative texts. I love and value the stories in which asides lead to more asides, tangents lead to more tangents, oftentimes with no hope of returning to the original narrative. Consider that sometimes, the narrative asides and tangents are indeed the point of the story.

To be a poet is to be a very good listener. To be a poet is to piece together some kind of musical or artful narrative from official and unofficial documents and undocuments, and to do so in all languages available to me. Most importantly, I have come to know that some stories take decades before they are ever told, and that in order for me to ever have access to these stories, I must offer something to initiate the exchange. I recently told my now retired mother about one of my dreams, in which her deceased father appeared. I told her this, not in any kind of formal setting, but while she was sweeping the kitchen floor. In return, she told me about how her mother, my grandmother, once had dream foretelling her own miscarriage. This miscarriage was not something I ever knew. Some stories must wait decades to be told, and when they arrive, they do so spontaneously.

None of what I have written here is specific to Filipino immigrant poets in America. But perhaps it can be said that my work ethic and aesthetic preferences as an immigrant in America emphasize exchange/sharing, hearing and writing multiple voices speaking simultaneously.

Notes

1. Arnold, Ellen L, and Leslie M. Silko. *Conversations with Leslie Marmon Silko*. Jackson: Univ. Press of Mississippi, 2000. Print. Reprinted from Iftekharuddin, Farhat, Mary Rohrberger, and Maurice A. Lee. *Speaking of the Short Story: Interviews with Contemporary Writers*. Jackson: University Press of Mississippi, 1997. Print. pp. 237–247.

Unconventional Bonds
Writing Through Dementia and the Borderless Trauma of War
Ocean Vuong

I'm lying in bed on a rainy night in Brooklyn. Lightning lights the silhouette of an oak tree outside my window, its twisted branches rinsed with rainwater. Like any other thunderous night, I am waiting for her to cry—for her voice to break through the dark hallway and into my room. And sure enough, by the third crashing thunderclap, a sharp wail shoots through the house, reverberating in my bedsprings. I bury my face into the blanket and curl into myself, hoping she will calm and return to sleep as she tends to do on calmer nights. But this isn't one of those nights. Within minutes, my bedroom door bursts open and the shade of a small woman collapses onto the hardwood, screaming and writhing on a square of light fallen through the window. I leap from the mattress and gather her frail body into my arms. I stroke her back, my fingers frantically rubbing the length of her arm, trying to coax her back to the present, to herself. This isn't a nightmare. The woman is eighty-four-years old and suffers from severe dementia. Her name is Grazina (pronounced Gra-jzeen-na) and she is my landlady—sort of.

I take care of Grazina in lieu of paying rent. It's the only way I manage to live and write in New York City on my own. Like most young writers before me, I came to the city hoping to better inform my art. But, more practically, I came to the city to go to school. My single mother, being an immigrant from Vietnam and living in a housing project in Hartford, Connecticut, cannot afford to pay for my education let alone support my vague ambition to become a writer. As the oldest son in a Vietnamese household, it's my "filial duty" to obtain an education and provide a house, a home for my mother to grow old in. It's a responsibility I accept and embrace with pride.

*

I am able to attend university only because of a generous scholarship from Brooklyn College. Unfortunately, the scholarship doesn't come with an apartment to accommodate living in one of the most expensive cities in the world. When I first arrived in New York City in the fall of 2008, I had exactly $564.00 in my checking account and a backpack jammed-full of handwritten poems. Other than a few distant acquaintances in the city, I knew no one. Through the generosity of a few kind folks I did know, however, I was able to set up an intricate couch-surfing map that stretched across three boroughs, with the occasional night in Hoboken, New Jersey. I ended up sleeping on three different couches in addition to the tiled corner of a kitchen each week. I showered wherever and whenever I could. Of course, there were nights when my host could not accommodate me: relatives were visiting, landlord checking in, vacations, illness, etc. But I was usually quite crafty and found last minute accommodations from other friends, sometimes even strangers I met at various poetry readings or open-mics.

*

One day after classes, I was making my way into the Starbucks outside of campus to charge my phone when I saw I had a missed call.
It was from a friend who lived on Long Island. I met him at a few
literary events I'd been to throughout the city. I had told him a week
earlier about my nomadic navigations throughout the city. Shocked,
he suggested I just return to Hartford, or at least call my mother.
But neither was a plausible option. Calling my mother and telling
her I was semi-homeless would only cause her to worry. She would
frantically wire me the little money she had in her tip jar at the nail
salon she worked at and spend days preparing my favorite dishes to
welcome me home. And although I was often tempted to do so, the
semester was already in its fourth week and I figured I could just
"tough it out" and at least get twelve credits closer to my degree.
Besides, my mother was so proud of having a son attend college.
I couldn't stomach disappointing her. She taped a postcard above
her table at work depicting the gold-plated bell tower on top of the
Brooklyn College library and, not being able to pronounce the name
of the school, would gleefully point to the card when customers and
co-workers inquired about her oldest son. "My son in the college!
He go here! New York City."

   I called my friend back. "I have a deal for you," he said, "take care
of my grandmother in Brooklyn and you get a room for free…"
The words "room" and "free" were all I remembered hearing. "Can
I come now? … Okay. I'll be there in an hour. Wait, wait—what train
do I take?"

   The building was an old Brooklyn brownstone: two floors and
three rooms, only one of which was occupied. The children had
long moved out and the husband long passed away. When my

friend opened the door, a little puff of white hair hovered behind his shoulder. An old woman timidly peered out from behind him. Slowly, she stepped out from behind my friend and started to smile, apparently relieved at my small stature. "Oh, he's just a small one! That's good! That's good. Come in, we have tea." She turned in and I followed them inside the house. "Labas!" (Lithuanian for Hello), "I'm Grazina!" Her bright eyes were magnified by her thick glasses. She looked like a grandmother from a Japanese anime cartoon. I liked her immediately.

"Labas! I'm Ocean!" This one word would play a major role in our exchanges with one another. To make her feel at ease, I would always use her native tongue and say "Labas" instead of "Hello." For some reason, she never trusted herself calling me Ocean, perhaps because my name is more unique than what she's used to. And, being self-conscious about her dementia, she would say "Ocean" and quickly look down at the floor, thinking she had said something terribly idiotic. Eventually, she just called me Labas and to keep it simple, I called her Labas as well. From then on, we would greet each other by saying "Hi, Labas!"

She reached out and held my hand with both of hers. I almost pulled back at how cold they were. She led me through the dark hallway, which opened to a stuffy living room furnished with what seemed to be everything made before 1965. The walls were plastered with some sort of faux woodgrain. There was an assortment of odd, Victorian style chairs that faced no particular direction. Everything, save for the rug and our bodies, was coated in a thin or thick layer of dust. What was most bizarre, however, was a glass armoire in the dining room housing a fleet of sad-looking owl figurines also filmed with dust. In fact, there were owls everywhere. Apparently, Grazina is an avid collector of all things owl: owl clocks, owl paintings, owl lamps, towels imprinted with owls, even owl slippers. Everywhere I went, I was watched by hundreds of mournful yellow eyes.

She had me and my friend sit down in the old kitchen while she made tea. Fumbling through the drawers and opening and closing random cupboards, she tried, with great difficulty, to find the proper cups. Her breaths grew heavy and her poof of white hair trembled in the effort. "I know they're here. Don't—don't worry. I know … I know. Please …" Growing uneasy, I looked to my friend who looked equally confused. Finally, she turned to us; a wooden spoon and a sponge in her hand, her forehead jeweled with sweat. She had the look of a child who's just been caught drawing on the wall, waiting for either an affirmation or scolding. She was clearly lost. I suddenly realized how serious her dementia really was. Still, I was too excited about the promise of a room of my own that I quickly brushed it aside.

My friend took me to my room on the second floor. When I opened the door, I was immediately plunged into a thick musty odor. It was the scent of air trapped for too long. My friend walked over and opened the window, which had a picturesque view of the red brickwork on the side of the next building. Of course, I didn't mind any of this. After all—I wasn't actually living in luxury at my previous residences, which, for two and a half weeks, included a stint in Penn Station (but we'll save that for another essay). Then, I saw it: an old wooden thing in the corner with only three and a half legs. A desk, lit with a small square of evening light falling through the window: a blank sheet of paper burning on its surface. "Can I keep that?" I asked, pointing at the sad-looking yet invaluable arti-fact. "If you want," my friend shrugged, "I don't see why not. It'd be a pain to move it anyways." I walked over and touched it, ran my fingers across the surface, the dust, the bolts, the cracks and seams and knots in the wood, I opened the drawers, I sat down and placed my hands and elbows on the table, testing the height for writing. It was fake oak—laminated to look natural, but it was perfect. Perfect not because of its quality (or lack there of) but because it was mine. My first desk. It didn't occur to me until then that having a desk of my own, something I did not have even in Connecticut, somehow legitimized my identity as a writer. It was a badge, a label, a dedication. And, having no publication and barely any respectable poems, the desk was also an anchor, the promise of possibilities, that good work would be done, and it would be done right here.

*

A thunderclap erupts through the night, and in a small room in Brooklyn, Grazina's mind is firing a memory from 1944—in Dresden, where, as a teenaged girl, she and her family were caught in one of the most devastating bombings of World War II. Grazina's family had been fleeing the Red Army and was heading east when Allied bombs started to fall on Germany. The genesis of my own family began in the very nucleus of bombs. As a product of the war in Vietnam, my mother is a "con lai" or "mixed child" whose father was an American vet. Without the war, I wouldn't even exist. It's a hard pill to swallow and I'm not sure I've got it down. When heavy fighting tore through her small farming village, my grandmother took my mother, only a toddler then, and fled to Saigon. The city was supposed to be the most heavily fortified city south of the seventy-sixth parallel, the line that divided North from South Vietnam. Saigon was a merciless place in time of war, especially for a young woman with no education and an extra mouth to feed. Like many other young women from the countryside, my grandmother took to the streets where many American G.I.'s were desperate for affection and had plenty of money to pay for it. When my mother was born in 1968 and the family grew to four people, her father was already long gone—nameless and faceless.

I remember the first few years after immigrating to the U.S. We had no TV, no radio, and no one knew how to read or write in Vietnamese or English. The war disrupted everyone's education and all the adults in my family rushed into nail salons to earn quick, untaxable cash making other people beautiful. But even without books, we were filled with stories, and after dinner, we would all gather around my grandmother for "talk story." She would close her eyes, the words coming slow at first, but soon they sputtered and surged, always growing into some sort of song—a fractured folk ballad. It was as if pain could not be told in any other way, that only through singing, could the memory exit the burden of a body and flourish as something abstract and, therefore, tolerable. Within minutes, every wall in the room would melt into fantastical landscapes of terror and wonder. My grandmother would be in tears before the second verse, but always finishing the song between gasps for air. Her daughters would pick up the verse where they could. I hummed what I knew of the melody as fresh snow started to crackle against the windows and wind rattled the beams of our tiny Hartford apartment. We would sit deep into the night this way; surrounded by bright buckets of KFC chicken, the tea pot emptied and filled a dozen times over.

*

Living with Grazina had its clear advantages. Other than having a roof over my head, there is one particularly surprising bonus that comes with living in her house. Grazina's husband, Peter, who died in 2006 from a stroke, was a chronic hoarder, which might explain the phantasmagoria of owls, among other things, throughout the house (although Grazina insists the birds are a strict representation of her own aesthetics). One evening at dinner, over my steaming bowl of ramen noodles and Grazina's Stouffer's frozen meatloaf, she told me of how her husband would go on these long walks and come home with armfuls of odd items. He too suffered from dementia as he aged, and once, he came home carrying an entire front door to an unidentified house, having no recollection of how or where he procured it. Baffled, Grazina suggested he toss it out but he replied, as he always did, by valiantly raising his right hand to the sky, as re-enacted by Grazina, and saying "Don't you remember the war? You never know! You never know!" before proceeding to drag the door down to the basement where, it seems, everything was stored. Out of curiosity, I took a flashlight and went down to look for myself. I reached the bottom of the stairs and was immediately confronted by a life's worth of items: pots and pans, black garbage bags filled with myriad clothes, dozens of shoes, filing cabinets partly obscured by old and broken furniture, sewing machines (yes, as in plural, as in three!), a wooden rocking horse with one of its eyes gouged out, a box full of vitamins from the '70s nestled between rolls of condoms just as old. There was, however, a single winding path slightly wider than my waist that lead to a back room. I headed through and pulled a string that lit a single brownish light bulb. As the bulb swayed above me, casting my shadow back and forth across the room, I saw what appeared to be a huge library. There were shelves, stacked three books deep, that covered entire walls from floor to ceiling. The books were mostly pulp fiction ranging from the '50s to the '80s. There was also a back wall covered by a large black sheet. I worked through the dust, one arm over my mouth, peeling the fabric back and shining my flashlight on the shelf. As drifts of dust swirled through the beam of light, I saw the hidden books. They were paper gold. Rows and rows of western history's most timeless classics: Homer, Shakespeare, Tolstoy, Austen, Flaubert, Turgenev, Faulkner, even Nabokov, Salinger and Atwood. Most of the books were paperbacks, cheaply made from the '50s and were printed for vast distribution. But that didn't change what was written inside them. There was also the entire collected library of Steinbeck and Hemingway in hardback. My mouth agape, my blood pressure rising, dust in my lungs, I dove into the books. The years had glued the covers together, and, as I attempted to dislodge them from the shelves, some books came out attached in twos, even threes. Others were eaten, almost entirely, by rats. I lifted a trio of Camus's books and peered into a golf ball-sized hole burrowing right through three existentialist masterpieces—cover to cover. Luckily, there were often duplicate copies of the books and I managed to salvage both *The Stranger* and *The Rebel*, among other modern classics despite the decades of rodent feasting. And since I had no TV and certainly no Internet connection, the secret library became my new pleasure. I would finish a book, return it, and grab another from the shelf, making my way through centuries of great literature. I would stay up deep into the night, often holding vigil over Grazina's volatile dementia attacks, the pages of *Crime and Punishment* ringed with mold and falling apart in my hands. I would turn a page and it would break off, the book literally disintegrating as I read it. When I finished, there was only a single back cover between my fingers. It proved to be one of the most invaluable experiences in my nascent life as a writer.

*

With Grazina, most of my duties are manageable. I am in charge of her pills, which means I have to know what they look like and remember their names—all fourteen of them. She needs pills for everything from cholesterol, to arthritis, to nerves, to dementia, and even one for "general pain." I have to allocate the pills into a giant plastic organizer labeled with the time and days of the week, making certain she takes them at the scheduled hour. Missing one dose risks the possibilities of a severe dementia attack. But eventually, I got better at reading her body language and emotions. If she starts to talk to herself while watching TV, or if she just starts wandering around the house, putting owl figurines into her pockets, I know we are heading towards catastrophic possibilities. I can usually see an attack coming hours ahead of time and try to talk to her or put her to bed for a nap. But sometimes, it's a lot trickier.

One morning she was watching *The Price is Right* as I was leaving for school, and, as I passed her to leave the house, she leapt up from the couch and grabbed my arm. "Eric!" (the name of her forty-eight year old son), "you can't leave me like this! What did I do to you!" Large veins erupted across her forehead, her eyes widening behind the heavy glasses. "I raise you! I come to this country for you and now you run away from your mother!" This was followed by a slew of what I assume to be very harsh and desperate Lithuanian. She was so deeply stricken by the attack, that there was nothing I could do to convince her that I was, in fact, her twenty-two year old Vietnamese caretaker poet. With Grazina still clinging to my arm, I called her daughter on Long Island who promised Grazina that Eric was at her own house (which wasn't even true; Eric lives in Boston and hasn't seen Grazina in over 8 years) and that he was fine and that he would be coming home soon. "Are you sure, honey? Oh. Okay. I see my son later then." She smiled and hung up before turning to me, wrenching her hands, "I'm so sorry, Labas." "It's ok, Labas. But I have to go to school now. Remember, here's the OFF button on the remote control."

Other times, it's flat-out eerie: I came home one evening after a late night at the library and found Grazina sitting in the kitchen having a casual conversation with an empty chair. When she saw me she pointed to the chair and said "Labas, why don't you make some tea for this nice little girl here?" This was followed by me silently freaking out and ushering her into bed. Sometimes, to make sure her mind is working the way it should be, I check on her by asking her who the president is every few hours. Other responsibilities include showing her how to use the microwave and cooking for her, shoveling the sidewalk and driveway, getting groceries, fixing the cable when it goes out, teaching her how to use the TV remote, for the fourth time that day. Sometimes, while working on a poem, and, in the midst of wrestling a stubborn metaphor, I walk to the staircase and yell, "Grazina! Who is the president?!" "My God!" she would shout from the living room, clearly annoyed, "It's ughbama!" "Okay … Thank you."

Some of my favorite moments are at breakfast when she would read old Lithuanian magazines, sometimes stretching back to the '80s, while sipping her coffee. "You see this?" she'd ask, pointing to a picture of a young girl wearing a sweater with the neck buttons opened, "Who the hell is going to marry her? My god!" Or, I'd be reading poems or working on one of my own and she'd always ask me to read one to her: "Labas, read me a love poem, please." I'd read and she'd sit there, staring out the window, her eyes searching for some distant year in her long life, or perhaps simply blanking out. Whatever it was, I was always glad to see her pleased. When I finished, she'd look at me from beneath her glasses and smile, saying, "Very well then. Very well then, Labas." It's in these moments that I thought: this isn't so bad, she's actually getting better.

But then, here I am, the thunder growing louder, the rain relentless. Grazina is clinging to my shirt and, between gasping breaths, begs me to save her brother whose charred limb she sees poking out beneath a pile of rubble. She points into the darkness and her hand is swallowed by it. I can hear her wet eyelids blinking rapidly as the memory flashes behind them, so clearly that she reaches out for it, insisting that I too should help her. I try to calm her with words: "It's okay. It's just a dream. Please. I'm here. I'm here. It's Labas." But her terror is shocking in its vigor and determination. In my panic, I forget that she barely understands English. So I do what I know best, what my grandmother did for me on those hot summer nights when I was a child, lying awake wheezing and sweating with nightmares, I start to sing. My voice unsteady and crackling, I guide the dirge of my grandmother's lost country into Grazina's ears and through her buckling body. I sing, the long sad notes of ancient Vietnamese poets. And, after about thirty seconds of this, Grazina begins to wilt from her body's long and tarnished history and returns to the present. I keep up the song and can feel her breathing slowing, her clutch easing. My singing softens into a whisper and I stop to ask the crucial question: "Grazina," I say, willing her eyes to stay with my own, "who is the president?" She looks up, her face exhausted, nearly pleading for something to stop or begin. "I am," she says, "I am the president of this God-damned country. Ave Maria." She chuckles and asks politely to be brought to bed, and we shuffle down the hall and I assist her in, pulling the covers to her neck and tucking the sheets beneath her legs. I sit by her and sing softly the same song until I can hear her breathing evening out, lulling into sleep.

Despite the obvious confusion and difficulties of living with Grazina, not once have I considered it impossible. In fact, I see myself to be quite fortunate, blessed even. Here I am, an immigrant whose family, or what's left of it, has been living below the poverty line for over twenty years; I shouldn't be living the life of a writer in New

York City while having practically zero income. I shouldn't be going to a great college and studying with some of the smartest and most passionate thinkers in their fields. I shouldn't have the luxury of making the art I love and feel so strongly about. And yet, here I am.

Before I sit down to write, I always hum my grandmother's song, the one I sang and keep singing to Grazina. The simple ritual helps me focus my attention towards the page, like a call to prayer. I write because, at the risk of sounding naive, I believe in the unquestionable power of words, that poetry can change a life, perhaps not in that one sweeping moment of profound epiphany, but like the words we chisel into the page, our world, and the experiences we make from it, is changed through time, through that steady erosion and resurfacing of meaning. I close the door to Grazina's room save for a crack just in case she panics again. I close the door thankful I have a door to close, a room of my own, and a life that allows me the privilege to chisel away something other than myself.

"Labas?"

"Yes? … I'm here."

"Will you have a new poem for me at breakfast time?"

"Of course."

"A love poem, okay?"

"A love poem."

"Good … Good. That's nice."

"Okay."

"Okay."

"Goodnight, Labas."

"Goodnight, Labas."

V: A Third Space

Poetry as Country, Country as Choice

Lisa Birman

I started thinking of myself as an immigrant poet when I started thinking of countries as people. It took an absence from both my country of origin and my country of choice. I had to be in a third place, another. I never meant to leave Australia on a permanent basis. I am still unconvinced that I have. My departures from the United States were also temporary; teaching trips to the Czech Republic, visiting family in Australia, tracing roots buried deep beneath the ground of Poland. I was at best only half-living in my country of choice.

Throughout the five year cycle of visas, renewals, and green card applications, I didn't know where I wanted to live, I only knew I wanted to choose. When news came on February 14, 2006, that my green card application was approved, I drank champagne at Café Savoy in Prague, and couldn't remember why I left Australia. Except for this: I left for poetry. I left because the poets who called to me seemed to be calling across the Pacific Ocean. I left because I wanted to get closer to their voices. I wanted to hold their manuscripts in libraries. I wanted to study them in performance halls and coffee shops. I wanted to know how they lived.

I chose poetry and then I chose country. And once I was chosen back, I wasn't so sure. Did I really want to stay? Was it a betrayal? Was poetry worth it? I kept telling myself that I wasn't choosing the United States over Australia, I was choosing the choice. I was choosing poetry.

I was and am frightened by the documents of immigration. Every question needs such a specific answer. I don't have a terribly specific memory. It is too entwined with imagination. Perhaps that is a common problem for poets. When I went for my immigration medical, my tuberculosis test came back as a false positive. As it does for nearly every immigrant. A result of childhood inoculation. A result of immigration. My memory is also full of false positives. I kept worrying about being caught in a lie, in an act of imagination rather than memory.

None of this matters to the people at U.S. Citizenship and Immigration Services in Lincoln, Nebraska. They need their forms. As do poets. So for every form I filed for U.S.C.I.S., I also claimed a copy for poetry. I made black outs of their documents, I rearranged their words. I wrote them sonnets and list poems. I translated works by American poets and legislators. I turned to songs about love and about land and about what we will and will not do to keep them safe.

I had spent five years courting a country, and now that the chase was over I was not so sure about the thrill. As in all matters of love, timing is a question. I had come here in the summer of 2001. We suffered, the United States and I. It made us closer. It made us a unified pronoun. But then it changed us. We started keeping too many guns in the house. It didn't make me feel safer. It made me feel paranoid.

Did we even love each other, this country and I? Were we really compatible? Were we just comfortable? Used to each other? Was it too much trouble to break up? To break our newfound pronoun?

Relationship is a complicated thing. It is not only about the beloved. It is about the self and the beloved. It is about choosing. I didn't know what I was choosing when I moved here. I only knew that there was poetry and that I wanted to get as close as I could get to it. And when things went wrong, after the romance of it went a little sour, it seemed like maybe poetry was not enough, that we couldn't live on love alone. But it was through poetry that I learned to love the United States. I learned to appreciate its history, to question its choices, to expect it to live up to its best possible self. All of the things we expect in love, whether that love is a person or a place.

My America is a translation. It folds through my mother tongue, through the tongues of Australian poets, US American poets, through immigrants and citizens, through the lines on the page and the lines at the airport. And I still choose poetry as home.

Of Roots and Leaves

Sholeh Wolpé

I am part of all that I have met;
Yet all experience is an arch wherethro'
Gleams that untravell'd world, whose margin fades
Forever and forever when I move.
How dull it is to pause, to make an end,
To rust unburnish'd, not to shine in use!
—*Ulysses*, Lord Alfred Tennyson

I lost my country drop by drop of blood, brutality and intolerance.
Devastated that I may never return to Iran, I began a journey away
from that cat-shaped country on the map, away from my beloved
Alborz mountains, and cities brimming with history and songs;
away from that place I still see through my childhood's eye: a home
with a landlocked sea that eats shooting stars, and cafes where sto-
rytellers sing Ferdowsi's epic poems—a country not yet spoiled, rav-
aged or returned to a time of less freedom, less equality, less anything smelling of kindness and justice. I left my country the way one
leaves one's shadow behind; walked towards a new universe of my
own construct. I questioned everything in order to build something
new: a new country, a home, a place that welcomes truth, kindness,
and endless vision. But shadows have a way of following their makers; and questions can be more dangerous than facts.

*

On my fortieth birthday I woke up earlier than usual, had my morning espresso macchiato, toast smeared with almond butter and ginger preserve, glanced at the headlines in the *LA Times*, and wrote this poem on the back of a crumpled page:

The Painted Sun

A tempest is brewing in my pen
from which the ink of an "infidel"
is about to spill and stain
the walls of faith.

The turbaned owls of the crescent moon
the robed bears of the cross who have painted
the sun on the limestone walls of this prison
set fire to the air we breathe.

God weeps behind the mask tattooed on His face.

And with that, I jumped off the airplane of religious certitude—without a parachute. It was the longest fall of my life. Scary, but exhilarating. Adrenalin pumped so high it was as if I'd injected myself with fields of purple opium poppies. Every minute stretched out into days as I examined my life in replays, pauses, and rewinds ... all my wanderings between Iran, Trinidad, England, and the U.S.—as an immigrant, an outsider, the "other."

My father sent me away from Tehran because I asked too many questions to which there were no exact answers—there were laws to be obeyed, requirements to be fulfilled. He sent me away because he loved me.

The night before I flew to Port of Spain, my mother took me to the flat rooftop of our house where we slept on warm summer nights. Under a waning moon and few large stars she held me in her arms. I still remember the softness of her breasts, warm under her cotton nightgown. She cried, said, *it isn't too late, let's unpack your bags.* Poor mother. She loved me in her own way. But I was thirteen, and out there a shining new world beckoned. How was I to know that I would never return to my childhood home? That it would be taken from us by laws legislated to punish "heretics" like my father.

Decades later, despite everything I had done, seen, read, written and absorbed, I was still asking too many questions to which there were no simple answers; except that now I was wrestling a beast, that creature we call organized religion and its powerful deity/idol/god. Had I finally gone too far? Who in her right mind jumps off a comfortable plane bound for heaven? Even if the destination is bogus, why not enjoy the ride and hope that something benevolent waits at the journey's end—even if it is eternal sleep? Whom could I blame? Surely, not my parents. By denying that there is only one "truth", was I going straight to hell and into the forever-company of religious zealots and their turbaned leaders who have taken my childhood home and country away from me? Or someplace more intimate and far more frightening: nowhere at all.

I took out my phone in midair and dialed everyone in its memory. Aunts and uncles, friends and strangers, wrong numbers with Spanish speakers on the other end, even telemarketers with sad robot voices. Could anyone make sense of what was happening to the world, to me? I craned my neck, squeezed shut my eyes and listened.

Mumbo jumbo. Static. Yaddi daddi da. Same old, same old.

Even the telemarketers had opinions that fell within the circles of "right" and "wrong" drawn on the yellowing canvas of staunch belief or anti-belief. I thought of the time the president of the Atheist Society in New York, who upon overhearing my casual statement that I may be an atheist, had boldly strutted up to our table at the restaurant and invited me, an un-chewed piece of spicy chicken in my mouth, to the Society's next meeting.

No one grasped that I was calling for help from midair, freefalling towards the hard ground, or worse, the sharp tip of an unnamed mountain waiting to impale my liver. (But, Sholeh, why such utter desperation? Why did it matter so very much to acquire peace of mind before your blood became lava?)

Then, a sudden clarity: What folly! What grand self-deception to replace one certainty with its twin brother; to release one foot from a blue trap to only plunge the other in a green one like that proud atheist in that New York restaurant, imagining himself "free."

Uncertainty. What a mouthwatering, mind-stretching, monumental word.

First, there is the "un" which is always a great beginning for any word, especially one with such self-righteous ancestors as *certanus* and *certus*, meaning: sure, and fixed.

Second, the moment the nectar of that gorgeous polysyllable (un-cer-tain-ty) absorbs into one's blood, the mind's prejudice against possibilities catapults out into space, never to return.

I pondered. (This, still freefalling.) Wasn't that how I had come to terms with who I was without a homeland? Hadn't that loss birthed the writer who had carved her way out from between my ribs?

Cures are poisons that either kill, or heal. Balance is everything.

Listen, I was born into this world with a song. My aunt, a midwife, tempted me out of my mother's womb, singing of love, light and a kind moon. That's what I heard in my freefall when I was only inches from the ground; her voice; landed into my aunt's soft upturned palms, naked as the day I was born.

The key had turned, the shackles had fallen away; *uncertainty* unfolded into possibilities; cushioned a hard fall. Suddenly, boundless bounties: merging with the eyes of a tree, the ears of a gnat, that small sound inside the throat of an injured bird. I became water between rock and rock—fluid and flowing, always towards *away*.

Today, I am a writer in the world.

This is (not) my country. This is (not) my God. This is (not) my profession. This is (not) my flag. This is (not) my religion. This is (not) my race. (Ask: is anything yours?)

My soul, perhaps. The words under my tongue.

They call me an immigrant writer when I am a native of this land, these forests, deserts, this sky with all its pinhole lights. The "otherness" in their eyes is the space between my fluidity and the solidity of everything else, like water traveling through a mountain crack. Listen to how I was sung into this world, to how I now sing my own song, a part of the whole, not an alien to them, or you, but as fire is to ash, clouds to a deep well, or roots to unfolding leaves.

Contraband of Hoopoe

Ewa Chrusciel

For a Pole to write in English means more than simply a change in language. Czesław Miłosz and Adam Zagajewski, along with many other poets, claim that writing in your non-native language means death to your poetry, death to your culture. For a long time, Polish poetry inherited a Romantic tradition. Czesław Miłosz says: "What is poetry that does not save nations?" A poet had a special mission, a mission to save the nation. In 1795, when Poland, which was then called Rzeczpospolita Szlachecka (Nobles' Commonwealth), ceased to exist as a nation, only its culture remained. As a result, Polish poetry became inseparably linked to the issues of patriotism and communal matters. As a poet, by writing in English, does that mean I am casting off my own culture's missionary cloak?

To me Polish brings the smell of white pines, bristling snow on the Tatra Mountains. It is the language of oak—harsh, robust, sturdy. I hold the touch of this bark (kora) until cortex transforms into Kore, the abducted maiden of Greek myth, in my native lungs. I become a maiden examining forget-me-nots, a maiden abducted into an underworld of roots, from the roots of Polish to the roots of English.

Writing in two languages creates bewilderment for us and for our readers. It changes us. It transports us to new places. This miraculous transport, this bilocation, is one of the theological meanings of translation. In theology, translation implies the act of miraculous displacement, just like in Nicolas Poussin's 1630s painting "The Translation of St. Rita of Cascia." St. Rita is miraculously transported to a place where she desired to be. Perhaps writing poems is always an experience of migration, if not exile. It is, after all, a way of being in two places at once.

HOMING   INSTINCTS

Ornithologists say white-feathered pigeons are masters of survival. While I was giving a reading in Chicago, on Jan 28th at 5 pm, the roof of the pigeon exhibit in Chorzów, Poland collapsed under the weight of snow. 63 people died. Słowo nie zagruchotało. To tylko dach gruchnął. An iridescent audience on air. Archangels Barbs Homers Frillbacks Laughers Modenas Nuns Orliks. Swarming to the last of the roof. Dodging what is falling. Waiting for their owners in dead silence. While I invoke syllables, give offerings in Chicago. How un-expectedly something will rustle just a morpheme away. Poetry is a maker of white and the heaviness of white makes the roofs collapse. Brodawczaki. Garłacze. Latawce. Turkoty. Perukarze. Mewki. Pawiki. Błyskotki szafirowe. Poezja zawsze się spóźnia jak paryska dziewczyna na obcasach. Przylatuje na miejsce tragedii post factum. Poetry comes late like a Parisian girl in high heels at the scene of the tragedy post factum. Poetry, a prayer which saves only itself. Poetry arrives late. A pigeon that did not get back to the Arc but waves its olive branch from afar. And takes off on extended letters.

This poem from my first book in English, *Strata*, expresses my desire to be in two places at once. To bilocate. The Catholic Church describes the miracle of bilocation, which has been experienced by mystics, ecstatics, saints, monks, holy persons, and magical adepts, as the appearance of an individual in two places simultaneously. Writing comes from a longing for the presence of another place, for bilocation. My desire for linguistic bilocation is rooted in bilingualism, which means inhabiting two cognitive places at once. Bilingualism is for those who are unable to let go, who nest in two places at once. For those who dwell in impossibility. Poems bilocate to express what is ineffable. To give tribute to Mystery; to the insufficiency of any language. Bilocation saves us from idolatry.

As Costica Bradatan relates in his article "Born Again in a Second Language," when Samuel Beckett, an Irishman, was asked in 1954 why he chose to change languages, Beckett replied: "to be ill-equipped," which in French means "d'être mal armé." To be as Mallarmé? Beckett claimed that he preferred French because it allowed him to write "without style." Bradatan continues: "to abandon your native tongue and to adopt another is to dismantle yourself, piece by piece, and then to put yourself together again, in a different form." Bradatan also summons Simone Weil who considered the change of language as dangerous as the change of religion.

Let's take Joseph Conrad who switched to English after he moved to England. In his essay "Joseph Conrad in Polish Eyes," Czesław Miłosz writes: "a hidden complex of treason is discernable in some of his writing".[1] Conrad's guilt could have been awakened by Polish writer Eliza Orzeszkowa's article published in 1899 in which she accuses Conrad of treason for having forsaken Polish language in his writing. And yet Conrad never betrayed Poland. His characters embodied loyalty to a lost cause. His ethical ideas were condemned under the Communist Regime in Poland for being western, and therefore demoralizing, and Conrad ended up on a black list.

In one of his letters to a Polish acquaintance in 1903 Conrad wrote: "I have never separated myself, either in my thoughts or in my heart, from my native country and that I hope to be received there, in spite of my Anglicization".[2] Conrad never truly abandoned the Polish language either. By fusing two languages, he doubled two worlds. When you read him as a Pole in English, you recognize the familiar syntax and a way of conceptualizing reality.

In his book *Personal Record*, Conrad says that writing in English was not a matter of conscious choice, but rather an outcome of falling in love with English. He also claims that he did not choose English, but, instead, English chose him.[3]

How did the king of the English woods abduct me? To what sounds? 47,000 vowels and consonants stem and sprout from the root of one tree. How did I re-plant oak so it became an aspen tree? Aspen birches, like English words, depend on a disturbance— mainly fire—for regeneration. Yet they display wounds very clearly. Anything carved into them heals into black scars, recording the event. Aspen words are frail and solitary, yet they make underground passages.

Abduction is, after all, an ancient wedding ritual.

By leaving what you love, can you receive one-hundredfold? Can you gain from distance the places you have left?

In a certain sense, a writer receives a hundredfold by never being satisfied. In "Bilingualism, Writing, and not quite being there," Sylvia Molloy writes: "The writing of a bilingual writer is of need always altered, never 'disaltered;' always thirsty, never satisfied".[4] That thirst leads to smuggling. Smuggling has something to do with mistranslation and bilocation. Nobody knows linguistic smuggling better than those writing under Communist Regime. Writing somehow flourishes under opposition, if not oppression.

Compare this phenomenon to Kant's pigeon. The atmospheric pressure that seems to hinder its flight actually makes it possible.

Think of the Hopkins' windhover, which by hurling itself horizontally into the wind rebuffs it. Think of a kestrel, which buffeted by the wind emerges out of the wind even stronger. Polish writers, for example, had to invent their own code-language in order to cleanse themselves from the Newspeak imposed on them by Stalinist and Communist regimes. The communist establishment banned books which slandered the Soviet Union or any books which undermined the glory of Russia in general. Books that showed the West as an attractive place were banned. *Cancer Ward* by Solzhenitsyn was banned. Huxley's *Brave New World* was banned. All of Czesław Miłosz's books were banned. At a certain point, Lucy Montgomery was banned. Citizens' thoughts were banned. As a result, 2,482 books were banned. All the books written on emigration were banned. From 1944 to 1945 four and half million letters were censored. People learned to use a code. If a wife wanted to say that her husband was imprisoned for political reasons, she would use certain numbers or write "he was lately absent." In high school we smuggled quotes from Orwell's *Animal Farm*. All animals are equal but some animals are more equal than others. The noblest contraband dwells in fraintendimento, understanding in-between.[5]

Paul Celan used to say that writers are wounded by reality; therefore they look for another reality. What if some writers are wounded by their native languages, and search for another language? In *Lost in Translation*, Eva Hoffman claims that we can have a new beginning in a new language. We can be free of constraints and native inhibitions.[6] In my case, writing in Polish was always epigrammatic, constrained. Writing in English was explosive and baroque. Free of fear of making errors and experimenting with new material. Syntax in Polish was chiseled by years of Polish classes and exams written in Polish. Hoffman claims that it is easier to swear in a second language and be playful about it.[7] Have I exchanged the vocation for a playground then?

The price is the contraband. I am a smuggler of sacred sounds. Writing in English is the work of smuggling metaphors from one language into another. It is a work of mistranslation.

I am a smuggler because I do not like to renounce anything. I want to keep both of the languages and worlds. The price is the ceaseless border crossing, a constant mental shifting and shuffling between the two languages, between these two different conceptualizations of the world.

Here is my opening poem of my second book in English *Contraband of Hoopoe* published by Omnidawn Press (2014):

Can you feel the apparition? The hoopoe's wings beat under my blouse. The sound *udud udud udud* is tearing from my nipples: Pagan pole-dancing, my breasts have Turret's syndrome. My breasts are in flux as if singing church hymns kneeling down, standing up, kneeling down. I have to stop and soothe them with new lullabies.

The hoopoe is the dybbuk messenger chattering under my bra. This action is not unprecedented. King Solomon sent the hoopoe across the oceans to the Queen of Sheba to urge her with religion. Pliny said nothing about the hoopoe. On the other hand, Kirchen in his *Coleggio Romano* had a hoopoe in his collection of skeletons among bones of eagles, magpies, thrushes, and a Brazilian monkey.

My valley of deprivation, my cloud of unknowing, pray for me *upupa epops*. Convert me back to wonder. Cure my heart of such morbid desires to come home. It is you who take me across ocean, just as he once took all the world's birds on a

pilgrimage to Simurh. To a new land where jays are not jaded
and finches do not fling seeds at small children.

When I cross the border, I start hiccupping. The officer stares at
my nipples. I carry wonder inside me. I bring abundance. I stir
the wings within him.

Hoopoe in my poem is the other/Other. Edith Stein suggests that the
other puts us in motion, so we actively go out of ourselves to meet
the other. Emmanuel Levinas claims that the other is "not unknown
but unknowable, refractory to all light".[8] Levinas continues:

> But this precisely indicates that the other is in no way another
> myself, participating with me in a common existence [...] the
> Other as Other is not only an alter ego: the Other is what I
> myself am not. The Other is this, not because of the Other's
> characters, or physiognomy, or psychology, but because of the
> Other's very alterity. The Other is, for example, the weak, the
> poor, "the widow and the orphan," whereas I am the rich and
> the powerful.[9]

In the Hebrew Bible, the stranger is always mentioned in conjunc-
tion with the orphan and the widow. Foreigners are people who
cannot take anything for granted. Nothing belongs to them. To
paraphrase Jorie Graham's words: "They live in perpetual state of
adaptation and mercy. Their path is a 'twisted' one, a crooked path,
the one that takes you off the expected path—the one Mercury, or
Hermes leads you towards—'off road', 'off course', the left-handed
path the mystics would call it. You need to grow secondary limbs".[10]
Nancy Huston in her article "Mask and a Pen" writes, "foreignness
is a metaphor for the respect every individual owes every other individual".[11] Language is foreign to us, but imagine how one-hundred-

fold foreign it is when we grow up multilingual. Graham describes it as the strangeness that will not peel off: "One senses, as a child, very quickly the feeling that any word seems to somehow 'betray' or 'lie about' the thing it means to embrace. That there is a trespass here".[12] Graham adds:

> One kind of slithers around in various skins. What this leads to—and I am trying to describe the experience from the inside of the compositional process—(because I so like this question!)—is a feeling of not only hunting around as if with a sixth sense for the right word. How the poem's arc will unfold—in others words: where is the experience the poem is undertaking going to go? That is often, in some unconscious way, dictated by which piece of linguistic strata I am operating in—however briefly—if my English is "invaded." I always write in English, but these other languages carry in their marrow, for me, ages of my life when I was not an American, as it were, when "home" was a very different kind of time, when history, for example, operated as a very different experience—one of much greater duration and importance. If I suddenly stray into that place where the Italian or French are dominant, my sense of "what the issues are", for example, is affected. I might not even know it while it is happening, but it is happening.[13]

It is Emily Dickinson who demonstrated to us the strangeness of words. Words are multilingual immigrants as they constantly cross-pollinate and rejoice in multivalence. In her essay "The Wandering Bigamists of Language," Ariel Dorfman writes,

> If I am (tragically) optimistic about the prospect of bilingualism, it is because I believe that languages—in spite of an innate and inevitable conservative tendency that answers a hunger in us for stability and continuity—have themselves also always been maddeningly migrant, borrowing from here and there and everywhere, plundering and bringing home

the most beautiful, the strangest, the most exciting objects, learning, taking words out on loan and returning them in a different wonderfully twisted and often funny guise, pawning these words, punning them, stealing them, renting them out, eating them, making love to them and spawning splendidly unrecognizable children.[14]

Perhaps we—immigrant poets—do not write in a second language. We write in the third language. Rather, a third, 'emergent space,' a conceptual blend that arises from the oscillation between closural and a-closural tendencies in the text itself, as well as in the relation of this text to a reader's construct of the text. My first book in English, *Strata*, tries to inhabit this third space, in which closure and non-closure constantly flash into each other. It is a hybrid text incorporating letters and poems, as well as investigating the issues of identity, mediation, protest, Central European politics, and the Sublime.

That third language is also an attempt at bilocation. Out of two shifting positions, the third space emerges. It is woven out of bewilderment. Like Fanny Howe, "I am a victim of constantly shifting positions, with every one of these positions stunned by bewilderment." Howe defines "bewilderment" as a loss of one's sense of where one is. As Howe writes, "Bewilderment is an enchantment that follows a complete collapse of reference and reconcilability. It cracks open the dialectic and sees myriads all at once." It is resolving the irresolvable. Howe quotes Muslim prayer: "Lord, increase my bewilderment."

Writing in the third language is disorienting, sometimes disturbing. It recognizes the insufficiency of the native or second language, the human desire and inability to express the ineffable. Just to give you more of the idea, in Musical Variations on Jewish Thought, Revault D'Allonnes writes:

[W]hat is intolerable to Jewish thought is the idea that a being can die before fulfilling his destiny; the dybbuk is the spirit of one who has died "prematurely," and takes possession of a living person in order to try, as it were, to conclude his role, to round out his existence. It is not a ghost seeking vengeance or asserting its rights. It is a person making himself complete, fulfilling himself, wiping out the error or horror of early death. A phantom is hostile, ill-disposed, frightening. The dybbuk is good, it returns in order to do good; if the community wants to get rid of it … that is because it disturbs the social order. But, in doing so, it carries out the divine order. In this sense, which is the sense of truth, the dybbuk is an object of love. Love which is a scandal and disgrace to partisans of order but certainty and happiness to those on the side of justice …

So, my poems, as the critic Tony Brinkley suggested, are dybbuks. For example, in *Strata* my opening and closing poem "Na no la" is a haunted poem. It is inhabited by the lines and images that emerge and expand throughout my book. They perch on a log and pound. They form a drumming station. They become a ruffed grouse, pounding its wings until the forest hears, until the logs spark into lumen. By embracing both mourning and abundance, this poem also alludes to the title of my book *Strata* which signifies "loss" in Polish and "accretion" in English. *Strata* investigates the issues of bilingualism; the ceaseless border crossing, smuggling of metaphors; inhabiting two places at once.

na   no   la

They thistle in us. They speck in the morning. They tingle. Sorrelic apparitions. There is a tigress mother wanting to trim your hair. They come to us. Do you hear them? Some as heavy footsteps. Others—miniscule kisses. Thin as grass. Rising and

swaying parasols. They come with swinging hips. They come
as minnows. They try to get where they belong. They come in
wrinkles. They come as a host of molecules. They come as hard-
faced dybbuks. They swarm into this lighthouse. They have
fancy hats. With forget-me-nots. They pebble across the floor.
They fall from marigold trees and lie crucified on the road. Get
up and sing. They pinch like too much love. They trespass. They
arrive at a wailing wall. They dot. We are burying them every
day. We are burying them in staccato rhythm. They rise and
accrete. They beat electric letters in the air. They hop always to
a higher branch. They come invincible. They come to torture.
They come to soothe. They come for romance. They flip and
tremble tiny farewells. They come as mustards seeds. Do you
see them in a mulberry tree? They slide down the needles.
They come as growth on wolf trees, the dead winking. They
air the air. They come to forgive. They ask for forgiveness.
They come as hyphae. They come as hostages. They come as
clogged streets. They come in slow trains. They come as silver
jaguars. Burning bushes, doves, manna, the blood of horses'
necks. They come as purgatory souls. They chip off the wall.
In loops and whorls. They want to rent one line. They want to
breakdown. They re-colonize. They come to insulate us with
snow. They come in giggles. They come in almonds. They come
to eye us, inside our panther skins. We bury them. They come
in black chadors. They rap on our door with churned up grains,
tides, whispers. They come as drafts of juniper. They spread
on the floor as a cross. They are relics of grief and light. They
perch on branches like monk hedgehogs. They come as juncos.
They come in lekking crowds. They come in high-strung beads
and scatter into our vessels. They come in volcanic lavish.
They come as noble Odysseuses. They hover as hummingbirds,
calculating their rates of return. We bury them. They air the
air. They are ubiquitous as Tartar cheeks. They bilocate. They
come as yellow secrets.

So, yes, poems inhabit us, jump out of us like tigers, or dybbuks.
To quote Revault D'Allonnes: "Oh, good dybbuk, resting in my innermost depths, give me the courage to become you."

Notes

1. Miłosz, Czesław. "Joseph Conrad in Polish Eyes." *The Atlantic Monthly,* Nov 1957, p. 217.

2. Miłosz, 219–231.

3. Conrad, Joseph. Notatnik Osobisty. Przekład Hanna Pustuła-Lewicka. Czuły Barbarzyńca Press, 2014. pp. 19–21.

4. Molloy, Sylvia. "Bilingualism, Writing, and the Feeling of not quite being there," In: *Lives in Translation: Bilingual Writers on Identity and Creativity.* Ed. Isabelle de Courtivron. Palgrave Macmillan: NY, NY: 2003. p. 74.

5. Chrusciel, *Contraband of Hoopoe,* 66.

6. Hoffman, Eva. *Lost in Translation,* In: *Lives in Translation: Bilingual Writers on Identity and Creativity.* Ed. Isabelle de Courtivron. Palgrave Macmillan: NY, NY: 2003 p. 51.

7. Ibid.

8. Levinas, Emmanuel. *Basic Philosophical Writings.* Bloomington, IN: Indiana UP, 1996. p. 75.

9. Levinas, 83.

10. Biedrzycki, Miłosz. Chrusciel, Ewa. Interview with Jorie Graham. *Wiersz jest doświadczeniem pierwotnym. Fraza* 65-66/2009.

11. Huston, Nancy "Mask and a Pen." In: *Lives in Translation: Bilingual Writers on Identity and Creativity.* Ed. Isabelle de Courtivron. Palgrave Macmillan: NY, NY: 2003. p. 59.

12. Biedrzycki, Interview with Jorie Graham.

13. Biedrzycki, Interview with Jorie Graham.

14. Dorfman, Ariel. *The Wandering Bigamists of Language.* In: *Lives in Translation: Bilingual Writers on Identity and Creativity.* Ed. Isabelle de Courtivron. Palgrave Macmillan: NY, NY: 2003. pp. 36–37.

The Stories in My Ears

Vandana Khanna

Much of my childhood I stood on the edges of two different countries: the only Hindu at Catholic School, the only Indian amongst my friends, spending summers in New Delhi instead of at the local pool practicing back flips. I was pretending at "sameness" because I thought being an American meant having a name that slid easily out of your mouth, meant your parents didn't speak with an accent and your house didn't smell of curry powder and cumin. I was living "in between" hamburgers and samosas, jeans and saris, this new world of America and the old one that my parents clung to with every long distance phone call, every blue aerogram that arrived in the mail.

Growing up as an immigrant, I only wanted to belong: to feather my hair, to cut my name off after the first syllable, to tune out my mother's voice telling me I was different from my friends while she wiped the eyeliner from under my eyes. Writing was the only way I could weave these two disparate parts of myself together. Tucked away in a small bedroom in the suburbs of D.C., I would write on my mother's electric typewriter. I loved the sound of the machine when I turned it on, the vibrations rising through the keys to my fingertips, making them hum. I wanted to see the clean, black print stamped all over the paper's white sheen, line after line of words and memories that I had written.

Half a world away in another suburb, I was again standing on the edges: an Indian girl who didn't know when to touch someone's feet in greeting, who was stared at in the local market for wearing shorts and sneakers. In Delhi during the almost-daily electrical blackouts, amongst lizards clinging to the walls and street vendors calling out their wares in the tired heat of the afternoon, I would listen to my grandmother telling me stories of the gods and goddesses. She was trying to take my mind off the fact that I was sweating through my shirt, that I was thousands of miles away from anything familiar, that my parents had sent me to India for the summer so I could remember where I came from but felt like I didn't know where I belonged from the moment I stepped off of the airplane.

My grandmother spoke no English and my Hindi often stumbled from my lips, clumsy and uncertain with an accent that made my cousins laugh. My grandmother was trying to connect with me in the only way she knew how, her *Angrezi* granddaughter that she still remembered as a toddler sipping tea from her spoon. The stories and songs, the rhythms of those ancient poems half-spoken, half-sung in my grandmother's raspy voice bridged the gaps between country and language. I had a hard time translating all of the words, but it was the images of Durga riding a tiger, of a sky filled with burning arrows, and of a blue-skinned god offering wisdom on a battlefield, that I understood. Words into pictures, that was my first introduction to poetry, in the tight heat of my grandmother's bedroom, waiting for the familiar churn of the air conditioner to come back on. Because I couldn't read or write Hindi, those stories sung into my ears were what I knew of storytelling, of a country that I had left behind.

It's this early experience that has defined how I write even to this day. I need the words to live in my mouth, in my ears, to hum and chant and sing. I need to read out loud while I'm composing, word by word, line by line, trying to capture the rhythm and the story within the finite dimensions of the page. Each poem demands that I find the internal music lying within the words and its meaning. After those summers in Delhi it took me years to have the confidence to tell my own stories, to translate those experiences and allow them to be mine. Growing up, I wanted to ignore what made me different because I wanted to be the same as everyone else around me. Thus, I spent so much of my early writing life imitating other writers that I had little connection with, trying to deny where I came from, silencing the rhythms of the first language I spoke. It was only through reading Asian American and South Asian American poets that gave me the courage to write about what made me different, to accept where I came from and how I got to where I was.

Up until my first poetry class in college I had only ever read poems written by someone with a name like Walt or Emily or William. The first poets who showed me that I wasn't the only one standing on the edges were American writers who had come from somewhere else: Japan and Sri Lanka and China. It was my freshmen year, my very first poetry workshop where I was introduced to the poems of Garrett Hongo, Li Young Lee, and Chitra Banerjee Divakaruni. Lying on the floor of my dorm room, I pulled out a copy of Garrett Hongo's *The River of Heaven* that I had borrowed from a classmate and read a few of the poems aloud. I was immediately aware of the power, of the possibilities of writing from one's own experiences. From then on, I tried to find every Asian American poet I could to read. This was my own personal education as a writer, a journey from my grandmother's house thousands of miles away to my own tiny dorm room in Virginia.

Chitra Banerjee Divakaruni's *Leaving Yuba City* was the first poetry collection I read by a South Asian American poet that changed the course of my writing life. Her ability to recognize the complex relationship between past and present, to describe shifting landscapes and countries, taught me how to write in my own voice about other cities, other lives, about an "old" world left behind that still haunted my "new" life in America. For the first time in my life I had found names and voices and stories that felt familiar. I found other poets whose grandmothers didn't speak English, who would have ancient songs sung in their ears so they wouldn't forget.

It was the voices of these poets who taught me that there was another America, my America, filled with spices and languages that were not the "same" as everybody else's. It was the poetry of where I was from, which was a place half way between here and there. And even though these poets wrote about their distinctly personal experiences, they all spoke to my own wonder and estrangement, to the "in-between" nature of my life and my poetry.

It has taken me a long time to accept that I can belong to more than one place, to a culture that is a blend of many different parts braided together. I have learned that drawing upon the stories and myths from my childhood brings me closer not only to the India of my past but also to the America of the present. I don't have to reject one to accept the other. Being an Indian American poet means I don't have to choose. I don't have to reject *dahl* and *roti* for a hamburger, I don't have to know how to tie a sari or practice yoga. I can write in the voices of the past and in the rhythms of today. Standing on the edge means I can take a look around in every direction and pick which way to go.

Selections from *The Pillow Book*
Jee Leong Koh

18. Mount Faber is a misnomer

Mount Faber is a misnomer for the hill by which I grew up. It is not even the tallest hill in Singapore. I don't know who Faber is, but the word has always sounded delightfully like fable.

I went to a very small school on the hill. Radin Mas Primary School consisted of two distinct parts, the lower grades at the beginning of a long flight of stairs, the upper grades at the end. It was enough to teach one about large ambition and little achievement.

About the efflorescence of Singapore poetry in the last two decades, the critic Gwee Li Sui is right. It is not the result of cultural change, certainly not because of government programs. It has sprung up like wild flowers on a hillside, and it may die without altering the landscape. The best of us still aim to be major generals of a reserve army, pioneers of secondrate products, prime ministers of an island. The dreamier turn to poetry.

On every visit to Singapore, I make it a point—of what?—to walk up Mount Faber, going by the road that winds Toyotas and tour buses up. From the top I see on one side the public housing estates, intricate and useful, and on the other the featureless sea. Caught by the hand of the hill, as if thrown there by a storm, lodges a boat. To

the hungry eye it is a seafood restaurant. To the hungrier eye it is
an ark. I look at the sea again and now I see the ships on the mauve
horizon. I recite quietly a tanka composed a while ago:

> Because this country has no mountains, we think highly of
> hills; look, we point to the peaks, where we can live.

21. Happiness

I wrote this haiku for Kimiko's workshop:

> An old man
> walking an old dog.
> Rain tonight.

Reading it again this morning with a great deal of self satisfaction,
I remember the poem by Wallace Stevens "Description Without
Place." My pleasure reddens into happiness.

25. Why I moved to the United States and not the United Kingdom

When I walked into McDonalds in Welshpool, the floor sucked
at my sneakers. The server would rather rib his friend who came
in after me than take my order. He gave me a cheeseburger when
I asked for a quarterpounder with cheese. He counted my change
laboriously. The fries must have sat in the sieve since morning.

That was in 2002, when the Queen celebrated her Golden Jubilee,
New Labour was losing its shine, and Nelson Mandela called Tony
Blair "America's Foreign Minister." When I walked out of that joint,
I had made up my mind to go where real power resided.

Since then I have discovered that the superpower does fast
food badly too. That the corner where McDonalds is done the way
McDonalds should be done is Singapore.

26. Things Out of Place

A flute in a trumpet case. Red wine on white linen. Sprays of heath in a blue bucket outside a Korean deli. A cheeky boy among mourners at a wake. A beautiful man married to a woman. A Singaporean in New York. The Singaporean in Singapore.

The moon in a lake.

27. The Public Service Commission

They have seen us all, these six men who interview the brightest in Singapore to decide on scholarships. Civil servants, military officers, and business leaders, they could have sat in that formidable row for thirty years, just as we, alone on the other side of the long table, are in a certain sense interchangeable. The idea does not diminish them or us.

But I am asking their support for changing me. I am asking for the Lee Kuan Yew Scholarship to become a poet. I explain it is time to develop more than factories, battalions and public housing, it is time to develop a language of our own.

They are not impressed. They can see through me. They know that I will quit Singapore for the States, that I am a queer one.

What they cannot see is that working in a rented room in Queens I write by the light of Singapore, a tall yellow streetlamp with its cloud of flying insects. Rallying my troops with Matisse's fighting words—to be a force that cannot be dismissed—I fear that, like my country, I am too small to survive. Even when I dream, like Keats, to be numbered among the English poets, I am making into an Abbey the mysterious power station in which my father worked for thirty years but I have never seen.

The Reader Within Me
Majid Naficy

In the triangle of author, text, and reader, the reader has a divine power. If one does not pick up the text, nothing comes alive and the author remains trapped in the lifeless letters of the text. Moreover, the reader's role does not begin when a text is finished. As soon as authors pick up pens, they have their readers in mind, and the image of the reader never vanishes during the writing process. Every author has a reader within who not only knows the art of listening, but also speaks and, like a child's imaginary playmate, sometimes even has a name.

When I fled my country, Iran, in 1983, I brought my reader along with me. As a political refugee, I started to experience new things in Turkey, France, and then America. But for half a decade, when I picked up my pen, as a writer and as a poet, I was driven to write for that reader. Although he travelled abroad with me, he still lived in Tehran, spoke only in Persian, preferred Iranian food, and thought within the framework of an Iranian culture.

A good example of this can be found in my second collection of poems in Persian *After the Silence*, consisting of one hundred and three poems which I wrote over the course of a four month artistic explosion from December 22, 1985 to April 23 of the next year in

Los Angeles. Except for fewer than ten poems, which I will discuss later, all of the poems in this collection were written about the Iranian situation in the past and present. The poet is still haunted by the phantom of the lost revolution, which was crushed by a new regime of religious hypocrisy and coercion. He tries to portray his comrades, who were killed on the streets or his wife executed in Evin prison. Moreover, as a thinker he attempts to break out of his orthodox Marxist thought, diluting it with humanism and exploring the meaning of every single philosophical and social concept such as "state", "labor", "organization", "progress", and "sexuality." My body lived in L.A., but my soul was still rummaging through the ruins of a lost revolution in Iran.

Among those few poems in this collection, which are related to my new situation as an émigré, we cannot find a single one which is not written for that Tehrani reader within me. In fact, I subconsciously wrote in such a way that I would not be perceived as an émigré. I sought this goal by either erasing the specific features of life in L.A. or by making comparisons with life back in Iran. For example, in the first poem of the book called "To the Sea", there is no specific trace of the Pacific Ocean shore where I was then living. It could just as easily have been written on the sandy shores of the Caspian Sea.

In another poem entitled "In Anatomy Class", dedicated to Dr. Karl Marx where I have tried to dissect his idea of fetishism of commodity, the reader encounters the familiar features of an American supermarket, like Lucky and Ralph's, but the imaginary dialogue with the producers of the commodities is spoken with a heavy Persian accent because the farmers who have produced the cabbages, cantaloupes, and grapes live in the outskirts of Tehran.

In two poems, "What People Might Say" and "Satisfying a Need", which respectively portray an unhappy marriage and a utilitarian relationship between two tenants sharing the same house, the reader finds hardly any reference to the specific situations in L.A. on which these poems were based. In the poems "A Letter from Iran to America" and "House and Street", the author for the first time uses the words "Los Angeles" and compares the way of life in the two countries.

Nevertheless, he cannot speak freely about his new experiences and forces himself to compare them with similar situations in Iran. In another poem, "Somebody and Nobody", the poet talks about the conditions of the homeless, but again the reader finds no distinctive trace of L.A. life, only a philosophical reference to the homeless as a reserve army of labor in a Marxist sense. In a long narrative poem called "Exile Fever", I see myself as a refugee and describe to my reader in Tehran the story of my flight to Turkey, France, and the United States. In the last stanza of this poem I subconsciously warn myself against denying my new identity as an émigré and guard myself against becoming a prisoner of my own nostalgia:

> In these three years
> My lungs became filled with fresh air
> But my exile fever still remains
> Woe unto me, if like a wandering gypsy
> I become captive to the cart of my memories.

It seems to me that, after this collection of poems, which I published abroad, the reader in me gradually comes to terms with his new situation and sees himself as a person living in America. He seeks to cherish both his cultural heritage and his new identity. In the collection of poems in Persian called *Sorrow of the Border*, published in 1989, the proportion of poems reflecting the new situation has increased drastically.

In a very long poem dedicated to my newborn son, Azad, not only do I depict my bilingual world by including quotations in English into the body of the Persian text, but I also see my son as my own new roots growing in the second homeland.

In the next collection in Persian, published in 1991, called *Poems of Venice*, the reader finds different aspects of life at Venice Beach, where I lived for seven years. A turning-point in this long journey from the realm of self-denial to acceptance and adjustment is when I wrote a long poem on January 12, 1994 called "Ah, Los Angeles" which was published in *Daftarhâ-ye shanbeh*, a Persian-language literary magazine, of which I am a co-editor. It starts with these lines:

> Ah, Los Angeles!
> I accept you as my own city,
> And after ten years
> I am at peace with you.

The reader which I brought with me as I fled on horseback over Kurdish lands on the border of Iran and Turkey has changed. He does not want to live in the past, and looks forward to finding a new identity here. Nevertheless, today I do not regret having written those poems about the lost revolution. I see in them not only myself but thousands of people from my generation who were executed or imprisoned as well as those who are still living in fear in Iran, or have fled abroad in search of a new life in freedom.

Scenes in a Journey Toward Poetry

Pauline Kaldas

The first poems I write that relate to my experience as a young immigrant from Egypt to America are short memory poems written in my freshman college creative writing class. One of the poems is about the neighborhood cat who stole our chicken. Throughout that class, I recognize the inadequacy of my writing. I'm young and perhaps my still growing understanding of the English language can only lead me to clichés and sentimental phrases. But when I submit these Egypt poems, the response I receive is more positive. Other students laugh at the chicken poem, and, for the first time, I experience the possibility of my writing having an effect on a reader. Toward the end of the semester, I have an individual conference with my instructor, Carol Oles. I'm sitting across from her, still young, deeply uncertain, but heavy with the desire to write. Referring to the poems I had written about growing up in Egypt, she says, "These are good. Maybe you should write a series of poems like this." Neither of us can know to what extent I will follow her advice, that this will be the pivotal moment that begins my writing career.

In college, the poetry I'm reading makes no sense. My teachers talk about the theories and philosophies behind the poems till the page weighs down with meaning I can't decipher. The only poem that catches my attention is "The Love Song of J. Alfred Prufrock." I don't understand it, but I like the way it sounds. The words form in my mouth, and I relish their rhythm like music that rolls and repeats, a pattern that seems to flow through rivers. I sense that Prufrock exists in isolation, and something of loneliness enters through the words that move across the page. I read it over and over again, memorizing some of the lines to repeat as I walk across campus, the only Egyptian in a college of 2000 students.

After a few more writing classes in college, I find myself in the library working on a story about a young Egyptian girl torn between two cultures. It's the early 1980s and I'm plucking words from a barren landscape; there are no models that I'm aware of and none of my classmates have comparable experiences. *Are these stories worth telling?* I wonder. *Does anyone want to hear them? They're too personal,* I think, and conclude that they can't be true literature. For several years, I stop writing.

*

While working on my M.A. in English at The University of Michigan in the mid-1980s, I meet Lisa Suhair Majaj, a graduate student in the American Studies program. She is working on her M.A. thesis, which focuses on early Arab American literature. Lisa's life as a Palestinian American has involved a constant crossing of borders. For the first time, I take a step outside of my enclosed world. As a young immigrant, I have grown up with a clear line between being Egyptian and being American. Inside, Egypt exists firmly in the language my family speaks, the food we eat, the other Egyptians with whom my parents socialize, and the values they pass on to me. Outside, I am timid, hesitant to plant my feet with confidence in this new culture that often seems to contradict what I'm learning at home, especially how to behave as a woman. Lisa and I spend hours in the living room of her small apartment, and I listen as she talks about being Arab American, the intersecting lines of identity, gender, and politics. Claiming myself as an Arab American writer gives me a way to declare my voice and enter into the conversation of American literature with a sense of legitimacy. Lisa helps me to see that my identity stretches across the two continents and the line between them remains fluid.

At the University of Michigan, I also meet T. J. Anderson III—a poet in the MFA program. Our relationship brings me back to writing. When he talks about poetry, it's sound, language, and form where he places the value of the poem. The possibility of experimentation, creating new models rather than following established ones opens up for me, and I begin to see the page as the canvas for creation. I'm wobbling through these possibilities one day as I'm writing a poem about the 1967 war in Egypt. "I can't find the words," I tell T. J. "I can only hear the voice of the town crier and my grandmother in Arabic. I can't translate." "Then don't," he says, "Write them in Arabic." I'm appalled by the suggestion—*no one will understand them.* I keep complaining and he keeps offering the same suggestion until my frustrations lead to transliterating the Arabic words into the poem. It works—and I know that I have found a way to use language beyond literal meaning. My poems are coming from a different landscape that lives in another language, and with each poem, Arabic enters my words—translated, transliterated, and even in Arabic script, the layering of language makes its way to the page. This intertwining of sound and meaning is the linguistic world I live in as an immigrant. I grew up speaking Arabic while attending a British English language school, but when I arrived at the age of eight in the United States, the English I heard didn't translate into meaning; sounds garbled together cluttering my ears. After six months of listening in silence, the syllables untangled themselves and I began to understand. But at home we spoke Arabic, and like so many immigrant children, my transition from one place to the other was marked by that shift in language. In writing poetry, I blurred the line and the two languages twined around each other.

While at the University of Michigan, I gather my courage and decide to take a poetry workshop. "The War of 1967" is the first poem I submit that has anything to do with Egypt. But the feedback I receive has little to do with the experience of war from a child's perspective that I'm trying to express. Instead, the other students' awareness of my ethnicity reframes me as the exotic—"You're from Egypt, how interesting. What is it like?" And in response to the poem: "Describe the streets, the houses—tell us what it looks like?" I plead that this is not the poem I want to write, but there is little interest in the words I offer on the page. They want a magical place they can enter through the poem. I leave that workshop angry—is this the only option available for my work? To provide a tourist brochure: come look at the people, the houses, the streets, and let me paint them for you with colorful brushstrokes, make them appeal to your naked eyes. I write the poem they ask for, but there is an underlying critique as I describe less appealing parts of my native culture—the pollution, the poverty, the hardships of an overcrowded and economically struggling city. They love the poem, but I'm not sure anyone sees beyond those picturesque images. That poem, "Home," has been published more than any of my other poems. I get requests out of the blue to have it included it in anthologies and textbooks. I have surrendered and allowed the poem to live and be interpreted by each of its readers. One lesson I took from that class is that as an immigrant, I would have to spend my writing life resisting being placed in the position of tour guide.

*

Returning to Egypt for the first time as an adult, I circle the immigrant experience—no longer a journey from one location to another but one that wraps around itself overlapping lives and histories. In 1990, I accept a teaching position at The American University in Cairo and spend three years living and working in the city I only remember from my childhood. I reverse the immigrant pattern, reconnecting with family I have not seen since I was a child, teaching, living in an apartment, becoming part of an expatriate community, expanding what it means to be Arab American. The words on the page fail each time I try to record my experiences. Nothing I have found in poetry taught me how to write this experience. I am static until I release the notion of line, stanza, and form and let the words spill over the page, floundering disjointed, traveling from long lines slipping off the margins to single words that hold their space possessively, moving from text to white space that speaks of what is missing, allowing two languages to collide against each other to articulate an immigrant condition that no longer fits into a linear pattern. It is during these three years that I understand new experiences require new words and new forms, an act of chaotic creation on the page to mirror the instability of a movement that circles around even for those who do not physically return to their homeland. As immigrants, we're always pulled back with news of family, political change, friends—those who die, those who are born—the tug of homeland snatching at us. This story can't be formed in stanzas of equal lines but must make for itself a new form.

*

While working on my Ph.D. at Binghamton University in the mid-1990s, I stumble on a class that includes several poetry books by women. For the first time, I read the work of Myung Mi Kim, Irena Klepfisz, Chrystos, and Audre Lorde, and I fall in love with poetry. This poetry speaks deeply and intimately to me, expands my life in ways beyond my imagination. Myung Mi Kim's poems float on the page, testing the edges of the paper and refusing to be confined by the space that holds them. Kim's poem, "Into Such Assembly" is a voice of resistance, asserting an identity against all the stereotypes, insisting on a vision of self that pushes beyond boundaries. Klepfisz's *Keeper of Accounts* draws me into a new understanding of what it means to speak the stories of others, how to talk of history, how to show absence and loss in the white space of poetry. Chrystos's anger awakens me to the power of that emotion, a new way of confronting the alienation of being misunderstood and pushed to the fringes. Lorde teaches me the empowerment of defining oneself and the multitude of identities a single person can choose to embrace as she calls herself "a black feminist lesbian mother poet." It is from these Korean, Jewish, Native American, and African American female poets that I learn how to write my own immigrant experience, how to see myself as larger than the world into which I was born. They give me new models and the courage to experiment, to find my way to a page that is mine to write.

*

Emigrating from Egypt to America at the age of eight, I'm part of what has been called the one-and-a-half immigrant generation. Those who immigrate as children arrive with identities partially formed by the homeland, but they are young enough to still be susceptible to the influences of the new culture. We exist between spaces, our lives a precarious balance as we negotiate an identity shaped by two worlds. Being a poet of this generation makes me look in two directions simultaneously. This is the vision I brought to the writing of my collection of poetry, *Egyptian Compass*. These poems speak of the displacement that comes with immigration: poems that delve into my childhood in Egypt where memory exists in images and impressions, poems of returning to Egypt and breathing in the sensation of a lost history, and poems that reach for that precarious balance. There is movement within each poem and movement between the sections, striving for a foothold that remains constantly elusive.

Where Are You From?

David McLoghlin

> "How many miles to Dublin?"
> "Three score and ten."
> "Will we be there by candlelight?"
> "Yes, and back again."
> (Nursery Rhyme)

I was 10 in 1983 when we moved to Darien, Connecticut—a town of large white wooden houses set far back from the road, a higher-than-average concentration of swimming pools and tennis courts among the trees. My parents didn't see themselves as immigrants: we had, after all, followed my father's salary to America. He was a lawyer with Guinness Peat Aviation, the world's largest commercial aircraft-leasing company at a time in the 1980s when Ireland's success stories were very few and far between. I remember standing barefoot on the white carpet in my parents' room. In the redwood quiet I opened their bedside drawer to run my hand through the casual brick of standby tickets. It was mysterious, and concrete: these were our tickets home, maybe I reassured myself. Through a later optic, it was like caressing privilege.

I remember a neighbour saying, "I guess you guys have immigrated, right? Have you acclimated yet?" (We would raise an eyebrow: "Doesn't he mean *acclimatised*?") The accent of the asker aside, even at 10 *immigrate* was intensely American to my ear—the way some words here can sound as if they were created out of Pentagon acronym soup. We didn't immigrate. In Ireland, the verb has been outward-bound for centuries; the exception being the 13 years from the start of the Celtic Tiger in 1995 (when emigration figures actually reversed), to 2008. When the boom busted, words like *emigrate* were waiting on the hook at the back of the door, like the work clothes of a previous generation that you've never worn, but that fit perfectly. *Immigrate* is strange because, linguistically speaking, *emigration* is home. Part of it also has to do with the Irish tendency to keep the compass lodestone centred where you come from. But whether you're five hours away or 20, whether you have to cross an International Date Line or not, there's still a ghostly jet lag of the spirit as you cross from the country where your daily life is, to the first country, where your life will become, increasingly, one of memories, the longer you stay away.

Of course, I only knew this non-verbally when I was a child. We'd lived in Brussels for three years before America, when Dad worked at the European Union (the European Economic Community, as it was then), so by the time we arrived in Darien there wasn't much of Ireland left to hold onto. Maybe that was why I sometimes pretended to know Irish (Gaelic). I spoke to my classmates in my own invented language, and they believed me.

Words were crafty devils in the beginning. Some enthusiastic adults said, "hi, I'm Randy! Good to meet you." This was great!—that people walked around saying that they were "horny." But if I said *millimetre* in school, the other children thought that was the cousin of the millipede, or just a strange invention of the Europeans. *Fall* was a new word too. On winter mornings when snow ploughs were out, and the light was a blurred white-grey, my mother would turn on the radio at breakfast, and I'd sit hoping for a snow day.

I loved the way summer smelled—like a merging of rot and growth that was almost tropical. I loved it if only because of the coolness that travelled within the humidity, like a sense of possibility. I liked the optimism of big fridges, the ingenuity of posting letters from your own letter box, how the postman drove a toy town van and wore shorts like a school boy, but I didn't like Tokeneke Elementary, where even some of the children who weren't bullies asked: "are there roads in Ireland? Do you wear shoes in Ireland? Are there tennis courts in Ireland?" Every time, the tone had a sarcastic uplift around the nouns in question: the contested articles of modernity. And, there was scorn when they said *Ireland*.

We had roads, but they were enfolded in the landscape, weren't vast-wide, and our shoes were plainer, less—sneaker-ish. We didn't wear sneakers all the time, not like the American tourists in white runners who were always getting in and out of tour buses in plaid golf trousers and the Aran sweaters they'd bought that day at Bunratty Castle. People laughed at them, because they were being ripped off. But, with the dollar's strength versus the Irish *Punt*, who had the last laugh on that one? Tennis courts were grass, usually. Our old friends the Eustaces had one at their holiday house in Donabate on the seaside in North County Dublin. It felt old-world and neglected—the net sagged: probably more from us jumping it than anything else—though the mythical good summers of childhood baked it hard. Not at all the courts of Connecticut, the Izod croc or Polo man that the other children wore every day. In Ireland in the 1980s these were clothes for the tennis club, which were relatively few, and smacked of upper middle class: rare, and rarefied.

Now I realise that my classmates' inflection belonged more to the mid-to-late 1800s than 1983. Though the time of "Shanty Irish" or

"Lace Curtain Irish" was long past, for these children of Waspdom there was something shameful about being Irish. Then again, since I never told anyone what they said, in my country-of-one I wasn't sure if it was being Irish or just me that was embarrassing. It didn't matter: whatever it was, I would extirpate it. I acquired an American accent within weeks, just as I'd learnt to speak like the English majority in my class at the European School in Brussels. The thing is, unconsciously acquiring a new accent isn't like hair colour. You can't expect it to come back the same way, especially when the original accent was severed several years and two countries ago.

When Irish people heard me speak, they said: "oh, aren't you the right little American now?" Although the surface of their saying it masqueraded as fondness, it came with a sting, a delighted passive-aggressive barb. It was always said with the surety of someone deep within the safety of the tribe: one of the little piggies who'd never left home, who hadn't had to question their identity, for whom identity was never relative or chosen. A subtle demarcation was drawn, putting you *beyond*. I would get angry, but not know how to express it. The double-decker Aer Lingus 747 was the only place I really felt at home. Tall, caring air hostesses served us drinks as the obvious emigrants passed through Business Class carrying guitar cases, like younger Luke Kellys. My emigration was incognito.

We moved back in 1985—not to Dublin, where we were from, but to Castleconnell, a river village 20 minutes north of Limerick City, and 40 minutes via back roads to the GPA head office at Shannon airport. Every week, the executives were closing big deals in Lagos, Jakarta, Asunción, flying on planes they treated as if they owned—which they did, in fact. In First Class lounges all over the world, the British and American old guard looked up from their *Gordon's* with surprise. If not unprecedented, an Irish accent with a power suit was something new.

The trickle-down was that sometimes, instead of taking the train to Dublin, we flew. Once, a helicopter dropped Dad off in the field next to the house, sending the cattle running for the ditches. Dad's immediate boss, Graham Boyd, was from England, and complained: "one simply *cannot* find an adequate supply of Fortnum & Mason marmalade." In Limerick, clothes were varieties of grey, like low weather. Among the Opel Corsas and Toyotas, my father's black Saab 900 Turbo may as well have been the Bat Mobile. As if confused by me, or getting revenge, people persisted: "so, where are you from, like?" Accents are the breath of where you're from, defining you in the moment of utterance. There are molecules and nutrients of home in an accent, like soil. But roots flailed in space when I spoke. Kids would push the issue: "you're English, right? Or American?" And sometimes I'd answer, "I'm from Limerick." But that wasn't true. Other times I said: "we're from Dublin, but we live in Limerick." And although that was officially true, I felt like an impostor. When I acknowledged that we'd lived in the U.S., they would nod sagely, with a kind of self-satisfaction, as if that explained it.

When older people knowingly sprinkled their conversation with Irish words, I smiled grimly, hoping they wouldn't notice that I didn't understand. I'd been given an exemption from compulsory Irish when we moved back. My 13 year-old self thrilled at it—*a free class? Four times a week?*—but in later years, a whole aspect of Irish culture was barred to me, and the exemption meant living without direct access. By 16, my map of Ireland was still almost all white spaces: destabilising gaps in the grid.

At school I was "Yank the Wank" for the first month, until I learnt a somewhat neutral, middle class Irish accent again. Sneakers were "runners" again, or "tackies", though no one said that at Glenstal Abbey, my boarding school that aspired to be the Irish Harrow, or

Eton. One morning in the refectory, the Junior Housemaster Leo McGrath called out during breakfast: "rugby jerseys are for the playing fields, Mr. McLoghlin." Everyone was thrilled with this. It was an inverse of the moment Eavan Boland recalls in *Object Lessons*. At school in England as a young girl, when she used the word "amn't", her teacher replied: "you are not in Ireland now." During the first week, when I wore a white hoodie with *Nike* on it in red, the other boys called out, "hey, Nike [rhymed with hike], pass the ball, Nike!" They didn't know it as a label; hoodies weren't common in Ireland in 1985. And as for the rugby jersey, I didn't know it was sportswear. I thought it was a jumper (Ireland), a sweater (USA): something I'd worn to school in Connecticut like everyone else.

*

I've now lived in New York City since 2010. I was 37 when I moved here to study Creative Writing at NYU: the same age as my parents when we moved to Darien. Like them, I didn't think I was emigrating. But two years have become almost five, and halfway through I met someone, a beautiful Michigander from Downriver Detroit. We fell in love, and got married. That is how I'm becoming an immigrant. With Ireland back in bad times, I sit on the plane beside young plumbers and electricians, their accents out of Offaly or Leitrim, who play Gaelic Football in Boston or the Bronx. I sit among the men who are emigrating out of need, and wait for judgement of my placelessness. It doesn't come, though part of me expects it. Another thing that's different is that the ambiguous privilege of childhood dislocation now feels like luck.

I imagined that moving here would reanimate that frozen place in my childhood, but it hasn't, not really. I didn't know New York then. We came in at most twice a year, at Christmas and for Patrick's Day (waiters with green hair; the clean, groomed tails of NYPD horses raising to let ochre turds flop down, threads of straw in the shit, like gold). Mostly, New York existed as a place of threat in 1983. There were glimpses of burning oil drums and scorched city blocks when we took a wrong turn looking for the Parkway to Connecticut, veterans in wheelchairs madly wheeling in to panhandle, glaring, their eyes lopsided and pirate-patched, turning the car into a fishbowl. The surface of New York didn't feel safe, though it was honest: as honest as a drunk man in leather trousers stumbling ahead of us at the Statue of Liberty, showing a builder's bum. ("Is that why Americans say, 'that guy's a bum'?") Connecticut's surfaces were beautiful but treacherous, especially at school.

Now that I know New York, I don't know Connecticut. When I took the train to Darien recently, to visit old family friends, though it's only an hour away, I found that my childhood is no longer there. Of course: that was 30 years ago. Parts of Darien, and Dublin—Dundrum and Donnybrook, where our grandparents lived, where we had lived—vague parts of Brussels near Woluwe Park already going snowy in a 11 year old's memory a year after leaving it: these were lit places in what was not so much a map of territory as an atlas of white spaces.

Now I know that moving from place to place as a child secreted its own connective tissue, slowly creating a country based on places and times that don't fully exist anymore—that do and don't exist—that exist in my head. The archipelago that memory makes: a private country.

*

In New York I've noticed that America at times wants an easy-to-digest Irishness, with charms that are lucky, and snackable, and smelling of green soap that is spring-like, and shamrocky. At times the United States wants Ireland's complexity reduced to Tom Cruise manically camping it up in *Far and Away*. Then again, for someone for whom Irishness is complicated, at least in my head, sometimes this can be a relief: if I want to, I can slip into a role. (In Ireland it seems at times that we ourselves perform Irishness to each other in terms of whose rootedness "in the sod" is more authentic: this especially with regard to who speaks Gaelic and who doesn't. One of the conditions of a postcolonial culture is that identity becomes relative: something chosen, instead of a fixed or given thing.) Indeed, for me to slot into a role would be welcomed in a city as performative as New York is. The thing is, having passed through the accents of our larger neighbours to the east and west, and back again to the mildness of a middle class Dublin accent that is sometimes not detectable in America, I resist performing.

My first inkling that living here might involve situations evocative of accent interrogation in Ireland came when an NYU classmate said: "you know, I sometimes forget that you're Irish." I smiled quizzically, thinking: "how am I supposed to answer that one, other than declaim in a fine brogue, *begorrah Your Honour, shall I dance a jig for your fine self?*"

Then he said, "I can't think of any Irish poets."

"What do you mean?" I asked him. "There's some living here right now: Eamonn Wall and Greg Delanty; Eamon Grennan has taught here at NYU; Eavan Boland and Paul Muldoon would be the most famous."

"Oh. You see—we think of Muldoon and Boland as American."

Mulling it over later, I thought: "ah, yes: the centripetal impulse, absorbing everything into itself—this is America." The other side of it is the United States' generosity in opening the gates of identity to immigrants. (Practical immigration issues are quite another story.) Underneath that capacious, overarching umbrella it seems to me that there are so many ways of being African-American, Irish-American, Pakistani-American, that America allows people to adapt their original identities to *here* however they want. (Again, issues of race are another story.)

My wife and I will probably live in Ireland at some point. (Hoping for the best of both worlds, we aspire to one day be able to "divide our time", as the most successful literary bios love to put it.) She will be welcomed, but she already knows that she won't be Irish in the way in which, here, I could "pass", and start becoming American. That isn't to say that the Irish aren't generous. To put it simply: rootedness in place is very important for us, as is origin. In Ireland, people who've moved the two-hour drive from Limerick City to a village in Cork, let's say, are still considered "blow-ins" 30 years later; whereas I've heard an acquaintance say: "I'm a New Yorker" when I know that he's from Iowa City and has lived here for less than four years.

At one point, another NYU friend said: "you've been here two years, right? You'll be an American soon." I was surprised, and demurred: "No, I'll never be American." Then I felt churlish, as if I'd refused a gift. I've felt this several times: the need to protect my "original identity", if I don't want it to be elided or lost under a subtle but powerful pressure to merge into the American story.

As a person it's important to me to maintain my Irishness (that makes it sound artificial—as if it was just a question of "lads" instead of "guys", or "grand" instead of "cool"). As a poet, it's doubly important to maintain and grow within contact with home. The person says: "If I become American" (doing so seems another artificial notion), "I'll lose where I come from." The poet worries: "won't I lose my inspiration?" It's said that Irish poets write obsessively about place: landscape as historical memory, or amnesia; as belonging, or alienation; or as site of ambush. Which leads to another issue: as the years pass and I write more about *here* than about *there*, what kind of poet will I be? Won't I be moving from writing about Ireland in the here-and-now to writing about an Ireland of memory?

Or, maybe living in the United States will free me to write about what I want, without having to be an italicised "Irish" poet. I have to confess: like most poets, I'm a hypocrite. I want it both ways. I want to be free of the constraining aspects of my tradition, but also free to use (or abuse) it in ways that suit me.

I'm not part of an American tradition, though two years at NYU has given me a schooling in American poetics. For example: I studied under Sharon Olds, but learnt more from her teaching presence than I did from her poetry. This was due to the fact that the middle "Digesting a Scorpion" section of my book addresses themes common to her work: the body, betrayed and abused, both sexually and psychologically. (Doesn't the former always contain the latter?) I deliberately held off from reading too much of her work until I'd finished the toxic process of secreting those poems, which she advised as my thesis. In the aesthetic containment of difficult subject matter she taught, I was blessed, and guided.

One of the unforeseen benefits of living here has been absorbing a certain cavalier attitude American poets have towards their literary tradition. If Irish poets have tended to write about place more deeply than US poets do, I sense that the Irish poetic tradition can, at times, condemn us to write about "Ireland" as a grand theme. As counterweight, the tradition in the USA says: "pick and choose", and reminds me I can write several kinds of poem: my Irish-person-in-America poem; my poem-about-Ireland; and the ones where those two blur, where it's simply a speaker, in a place, specified or not: not so much geography as soul landscape. I've started writing that kind of poem:

> Maybe the old man in Donegal tweed
> on the platform bench
> clear-eyed, with still hands
> among these anxious souls
> checking their texts, blackberrying,
> is almost an angel. For a moment
> he could be my grandfather.[1]

A confession: I positioned the old man as a foil to the "smartphonery" of the New York subway. I didn't invent him, though: he was a real person, though not my grandfather. American poetry, and partly all the Ashbery in the water—I haven't read him directly yet—has taught me: expand beyond strict autobiography; play and dream on the page; inhabit the dreams of a self who may or may not be you.

These are aspects of the capacious American tradition that I've grafted into my own. Then again—not to be difficult, but—I've never fully seen myself in terms of my own tradition, either. That isn't surprising, given that for many years I had a gap in my experience of Irishness, and probably still do. Before I began to explore that fissure through my writing, I felt homesick—particularly when I was in Ireland. There was a hole in the map, and at times it seemed there was no map. (The truism is nonetheless true: the psychic fault lines give birth to the need to create poems that, at the time of writing them, temporarily relieve the pressure. The old Yeatsian self-argument.)

By the time I was 18, I'd had a magpie education in three countries, but never the continuous narrative of an Irish National (Elementary) school education, where the same teacher teaches you each subject, moving fluidly between Gaelic and English. (I know that I'm romanticising it, and that several friends have envied the fact that I didn't have it.) Glenstal Abbey never stressed Irish history, or the study of Irish. In fact, Ireland at times seemed a condition to transcend. Growing up without Gaelic, without a coherent syllabus, or without seeking out books by Irish authors, and without much knowledge of Irish history before 1900, left me with an absence that itched like a wound.

In 2002 I was living in Madrid, teaching English to office workers during the three-hour lunch break. One weekend in May, my then-girlfriend and I took the train to Salamanca to stay in an empty apartment that belonged to a friend of a friend. It came to a head in a café in the old city near the cathedral. I was looking at the swirling red-ochre graffiti of the students of the 1600s on the gold stone walls—evidence of so much continuity—and felt the lack of my own tradition as a kind of grief. It wasn't that I missed Ireland. I missed where Ireland should have been inside me.

In the middle of it, I remembered my friend, the poet John Liddy, had mentioned the Irish College, and that I should visit it. (John has lived in Madrid since the early 1980s.) We found our way there from the Plaza Mayor, where people gestured over sunlit glasses of white wine, through quieter side streets. The Irish College is a museum now, though the museum part was closed that Sunday. The flagstones were full of weeds; swallows dipping around us in the cloister. There was nothing there now except for us, and my need for there to be an answer to the homesickness. There was a plaque in Latin and Golden Age Spanish: words from a royal decree four centuries before, honouring these "nobles Yrlandeses": these Noble Irish.

As I stood there, I started feeling my way back to the men who'd come to study the priesthood in Spain (during the Penal Laws, practising Catholicism was outlawed in Ireland); back to the rue des Irlandais in Paris; to running the three-legged race at Sports Day at the Irish College at Louvain (Leuven) when I was seven; to the Irish officers and doctors in the army of Simón Bolívar; and Sarsfield's Irish regiments in France. The Diaspora was there, starting with Saint Brendan's voyage to North America before Leif Ericson, and the monks who had reintroduced Greek and Roman thought to Europe during the Dark Ages, creating a way for the Renaissance to flower.[2]

In the Irish College at Salamanca, the question that had dogged me for years had found an outward form. It wasn't sudden, but something began unspooling in me, and I started to reinsert myself into my own tradition. It was natural that Brendan would be a presiding figure in my book, given that at least half of it explores what it means to be between, or trans-Atlantic. As a writer, my goal has been to find a way of being both: to be hybrid, to find a place to plant my trailing foot. As a person, I still feel the other foot trailing. It helps to remember that as a boy I was what's now called a "third culture kid", someone who transits between different countries, and feels that they don't fully belong in any of them.[3] I could have been an immigrant in the 1980s if we'd stayed on; certainly, I am one now. But immigration—leave there; move here—isn't a simple equation, nor the whole story. In part, I write to work that out.

Notes

1. From "Euclid Avenue", *Waiting for Saint Brendan and Other Poems*, Salmon Poetry, Cliffs of Moher, County Clare, Ireland, 2012.
2. See *How the Irish Saved Civilization*, Thomas Cahill, First Anchor Books, New York, 1995, and *The Brendan Voyage*, Tim Severin, Abacus, London, 1996.
3. *Third Culture Kids: Growing Up Among Worlds*, by David C. Pollock and Ruth E. Van Reken, Nicholas Brealey Publishing, Boston, 2009.

Contributors

Zubair Ahmed was raised in Dhaka, Bangladesh. Before immigrating to the U.S. in 2005, he was a professional video gamer for a year and a half. After finishing high school in a small Texas town, he went to Stanford University for his B.S. and M.S. in Mechanical Engineering. He is author of *Ashulia*, a chapbook published by Tavern Books in 2011. His first full-length collection, *City of Rivers*, published by McSweeney's, was nominated for a 2013 Northern California Book Award in Poetry. His works have appeared in *Tin House*, *Believer*, *Poetry Daily*, and *ZYZZYVA* among others. He currently lives in Everett, Washington, where he enjoys working his day job at Boeing and spending time exploring the Pacific Northwest.

Abayomi Animashaun's poems have appeared in several print and online journals, including *African American Review*, *Cortland Review*, and *Diode*. He is the author of two poetry collections, *Sailing for Ithaca* and *The Giving of Pears*. A recipient of the Hudson Prize and a grant from the International Center for Writing and Translation, Animashaun teaches at the University of Wisconsin-Oshkosh.

Lisa Birman is the author of *How To Walk Away* and *For That Return Passage—A Valentine for the United States of America*. She co-edited the anthology *Civil Disobediences: Poetics and Politics in Action*, and has published several chapbooks of poetry, including *deportation poems*. Her work has appeared in *Revolver, Floor Journal, Milk Poetry Magazine, Trickhouse, Poetry Project Newsletter*, and *not enough night*. Lisa served as the Director of the Summer Writing Program at Naropa University's Jack Kerouac School of Disembodied Poetics for twelve years, and continues to teach for the MFA in Creative Writing. She is from Melbourne, Australia.

Ewa Chrusciel has two books in Polish: *Furkot* and *Sopilki* and two books in English, *Strata* (Emergency Press, 2011) and *Contraband of Hoopoe* (Omnidawn Press, 2014). Her poems were featured in *Jubilat, Boston Review, Colorado Review, Lana Turner, Spoon River Review, Aufgabe* among others. She translated Jack London, Joseph Conrad, I.B. Singer as well as Jorie Graham, Lyn Hejinian, and other American poets into Polish. She is an associate professor at Colby-Sawyer College. For more information, go to her website: www.echrusciel.net

Kwame Dawes is the author of nineteen books of poetry and numerous other books of fiction, criticism, and essays. He has edited over a dozen anthologies. His latest collection, *Duppy Conqueror: New and Selected Poems* (Copper Canyon) appeared in 2013. He is Glenna Luschei Editor of *Prairie Schooner* and teaches at the University of Nebraska and the Pacific MFA Program. He is Director of the African Poetry Book Fund and Artistic Director of the Calabash International Literary Festival.

Michael Dumanis was born in the former Soviet Union and grew up in Western New York. He is the author of *My Soviet Union* (University of Massachusetts Press, 2007), winner of the Juniper Prize for Poetry, and coeditor of the anthology *Legitimate Dangers: American Poets of the New Century*. He lives in Brooklyn and Vermont, and teaches literature and writing at Bennington College.

Megan Fernandes is a South Asian American poet and academic. She received her PhD in English at the University of California, Santa Barbara and holds an MFA in poetry from Boston University. She is the poetry editor of the anthology *Strangers in Paris* (Tightrope Books) and is the author of two poetry chapbooks: *Organ Speech* (Corrupt Press) and *Some Citrus Makes Me Blue* (Dancing Girl Press). Her work has been published in the *Boston Review, Guernica, Memorious, Rattle, Redivider,* among others. Her first full length manuscript of poetry, *The Kingdom and After,* is forthcoming in Spring 2015. In fall 2015, she will be an Assistant Professor of English at Lafayette College.

Cristián Flores García was born in Mexico City and raised in Southern California. Her poems and essays have been published by *The American Poetry Review, The Rumpus,* HerKind.org, and others. She is a Fellow of CantoMundo, The MacDowell Colony, The Millay Colony, and the 2013 LetrasLatinas writer in residence, as well as a XXXVII Pushcart Prize winner.

Danielle Legros Georges is a professor in the Creative Arts and Learning Division at Lesley University. Her areas of interest include arts and education, contemporary American poetry, African-American poetry, Caribbean literature and studies, and literary translation. A writer and poet, Legros Georges has been recognized for her poetry and scholarship with awards including a recent Massachusetts Cultural Council Artist Fellowship in Poetry. Her poems have appeared in numerous literary journals and anthologies, and a book of poems, *Maroon,* was published in 2001. In 2014 she was appointed Boston's Poet Laureate.

Rigoberto González is the author of 15 books, most recently the poetry collection *Unpeopled Eden,* which won the Lambda Literary Award and the Lenore Marshall Prize from the Academy of American Poets. The recipient of Guggenheim, NEA and USA Rolón fellowships, a NYFA grant in poetry, the Shelley Memorial Award from the Poetry Society of America, The Poetry Center Book Award, and the Barnes & Noble Writer for Writers Award, he is contributing editor for *Poets & Writers Magazine*, on the executive board of directors of the National Book Critics Circle, and professor of English at Rutgers-Newark, the State University of New Jersey.

Andrei Guruianu, born in 1979 in Bucharest, Romania, teaches in the Expository Writing Program at New York University. He is the author of over a dozen books of poetry and prose, most recently *Body of Work* (Fomite Press, 2013), *Made in the Image of Stones*, and *Portrait Without a Mouth* (both from BrickHouse Books, 2014). Former U.S. Poet Laureate Ted Kooser has featured him in the column *American Life in Poetry*. Learn more about his life and work at www.andreiguruianu.com.

Philippine-born author **Maria Victoria A. Grageda-Smith**'s first career was in the practice of law. After marriage to an American that led her to immigrate to the United States, she rediscovered and pursued a childhood passion: creative writing.

Her first book of poems, *Warrior Heart, Pilgrim Soul: An Immigrant's Journey*, was published in November 2013 to critical acclaim. *Kirkus Reviews* spearheaded praise for the collection, describing it as "A cohesive poetry collection that … addresses fundamental issues of identity … boldly address(es) the beauty and ugliness of life … in grand sweeping language … (R)eaders will delight in … original perspectives on well-worn tropes … A forceful poetic expression of art and the self." She writes a monthly poetry column for the Chicago-based immigrant newsmagazine, *VIA Times*. Her poetry has been published in, among others, *Lyrical Iowa*; *Dicta* (the University of Michigan Law School Literary Journal); and other arts and literary publications. She founded and ran a poetry program for The Iowa Homeless Youth Shelters in 2007–2009. A featured poet at the 2002 Austin International Poetry Festival, she continues to read and perform her poetry in a variety of poetry readings and festivals.

Her fiction gained national U.S. recognition when her short story, *Portrait of the Other Lady*, won first place in a nation-wide short story contest in 2004. The short story and an interview of her were published in a Los Angeles-area newspaper. She attended the 2005 UCLA Asian-American Writer's Program and was featured as an emerging Asian-American writer in several print media and online articles.

Ms. Grageda-Smith has served as officer of various writers' clubs, conducted writers' workshops, and managed her own critique partnerships. In November 2013, the Filipino American Chicago Hall of Fame honored her with the Outstanding Writer Award.

She has an upcoming short story collection, *Pieces of Dreams and Other Stories*, and is currently finishing her first novel, *Gabriela's Eyes*.

Piotr Gwiazda was born in Olsztyn, Poland in 1973. Since 1991 he has lived in the United States. He is the author of two books of poems, *Gagarin Street* (Washington Writers' Publishing House, 2005) and *Messages* (Pond Road Press, 2012). He has also published two critical studies, *James Merrill and W.H. Auden: Homosexuality and Poetic Influence* (Palgrave Macmillan, 2007) and *US Poetry in the Age of Empire, 1979–2012* (Palgrave Macmillan, 2014). His translation of Polish writer Grzegorz Wróblewski's *Kopenhaga* appeared in 2013 (Zephyr Press). His poems, essays, reviews, and translations appear in many journals, including *AGNI*, *Barrow Street*, *Chicago Review*, *Denver Quarterly*, *Jacket*, *The Nation*, *Seattle Review*, *The Southern Review*, the *TLS*, and *XCP: Cross Cultural Poetics*. He teaches modern and contemporary poetry at the University of Maryland Baltimore County.

Fady Joudah's poetry received the Yale Series for Younger Poets and a Guggenheim fellowship. His translations of Palestinian poets Mahmoud Darwish and Ghassan Zaqtan have earned him several awards, including the Griffin International Poetry Prize. His latest poetry collection is *Textu.* He is a practicing physician in Houston, TX.

Pauline Kaldas is Associate Professor of English and Creative Writing at Hollins University in Roanoke, Virginia. She is the author of *Egyptian Compass,* a collection of poetry, *Letters from Cairo,* a travel memoir, and *The Time Between Places,* a collection of short stories. She also co-edited *Dinarzad's Children: An Anthology of Contemporary Arab American Fiction.* Her work has appeared in a variety of anthologies, including *The Poetry of Arab Women* and *Inclined to Speaks,* as well as several literary journals, such as *Mizna, Phoebe,* and *Borderlands.* She was awarded a fellowship in fiction from the Virginia Commission for the Arts, the Silver Award for *Dinarzad's Children* from *ForeWord Magazine* Book of the Year Awards, and the RAWI Creative Prose Award. Kaldas was born in Egypt and immigrated with her parents to the United States at the age of eight in 1969.

Ilya Kaminsky was born in Odessa, former Soviet Union in 1977, and arrived to the United States in 1993, when his family was granted asylum by the American government.

He is the author of *Dancing In Odessa* (Tupelo Press, 2004) which won the Whiting Writer's Award, the American Academy of Arts and Letters' Metcalf Award, the Dorset Prize, the Ruth Lilly Fellowship given annually by *Poetry* magazine. *Dancing In Odessa* was also named Best Poetry Book of the Year 2004 by *ForeWord Magazine.* In 2008, he was awarded Lannan Foundation's Literary Fellowship.

Poems from his new manuscript, *Deaf Republic,* were awarded *Poetry* magazine's Levinson Prize and the Pushcart Prize.

His anthology of 20th century poetry in translation, *Ecco Anthology of International Poetry*, was published by Harper Collins in March, 2010. His poems have been translated into numerous languages and his books have been published in many countries including Turkey, Holland, Russia, France, Mexico, Mecedonia, Romania, Spain and China, where his poetry was awarded the Yinchuan International Poetry Prize. He has worked as a law clerk for San Francisco Legal Aid and the National Immigration Law Center. Currently, he teaches English and Comparative Literature at San Diego State University.

Vandana Khanna was born in New Delhi, India and attended the University of Virginia and Indiana University, where she earned her MFA. Her first collection of poetry, *Train to Agra*, won the *Crab Orchard Review* First Book Prize and her second collection, *Afternoon Masala*, was the co-winner of the 2014 Miller Williams Arkansas Poetry Prize.

Jee Leong Koh is the author of four books of poems. His work has been shortlisted for the Singapore Literature Prize and translated into Japanese. A new book of poems *Steep Tea* is forthcoming from Carcanet Press (UK) in July 2015. Originally from Singapore, Koh lives in New York City. He is the co-chair of the inaugural Singapore Literature Festival in New York, and the curator of the arts website singaporepoetry.com.

Vasyl Makhno is a Ukrainian poet, essayist, and translator. He is the author of nine collections of poetry, including *Winter Letters and Other Poems*, translated by Orest Popovych (Spuyten Duyvil, 2011) and, most recently, *I want to be Jazz and Rock'n'Roll* (Ternopil, Krok, 2013). He has also published two books of essays, *The Gertrude Stein Memorial Cultural and Recreation Park* (2006) and *Horn of Plenty* (2011). Makhno has translated Zbigniew Herbert's and Janusz Szuber's poetry from Polish into Ukrainian. His poems and essays have been translated into 25 languages, and volumes of his selected poems were published in Poland, Romania, Serbia and the USA. He is the 2013 recipient of Serbia's Povele Morave Prize in Poetry. Makhno currently lives in New York City.

Gerardo Pacheco Matus is a Mayan native. He was born in Huhi, Yucatan, Mexico. He crawled through The United States' border at age 16. His Mayan and Mexican heritage influences his writing. He uses magic and history to bridge these two worlds that have been in conflict. His writing deals with migration's social and cultural hardships. His poems have appeared and are forthcoming from La Bloga Online Magazine, Grantmakers in the Arts, San Francisco Foundation, *Spillway Magazine, Transfer Magazine, El Tecolote Newspaper, Cipactli Magazine,* Amistad Howard-University, Blue Print E-Zine, "*OCCUPY SF, poems from the movement,*" "*Feather Floating on the Water- poems for our children,*" Poets Responding to SB1070, The University of Arizona Press, *Packinghouse Review,* and *The Los Angeles Review.* He was selected to participate and be a featured reader on "The Pintura:Palabra" National Ekphrastic Workshops, in tandem with the Smithsonian American Art Museum's Travelling Exhibit, "Our America: The Latino Presence in America Art." In 2012, The San Francisco Foundation awarded him the distinguished Joseph Henry Jackson Award. His poem, "The Children of La Frontera," was named one of the 2014 Best Poems by La Bloga Online Magazine *Floricanto.* His first poetry book, *This Is Crow Land,* should be published in 2015.

David McLoghlin is from Dublin, Ireland, but spent six formative years in Belgium and New England as a boy. ("Where Are You From?" is part of a memoir-in-progress titled *The Travelled Child*). He spent 2010–2012 as an MFA candidate in poetry at New York University, and now lives in Brooklyn with his wife Adrienne Brock, where they run the Eagle and the Wren reading series. His first collection, *Waiting for Saint Brendan and Other Poems* (Salmon Poetry, 2012), was awarded 2nd prize in the Patrick Kavanagh Awards, Ireland's best-known awards for a first unpublished manuscript. He received a major Irish Arts Council Bursary (grant) in 2006, and was the Howard Nemerov Scholar at the 2011 Sewanee Writers' Conference. His work has been interpreted on the stage and in film, and has appeared in Irish journals of note such as *Poetry Ireland Review, The Shop* and *The Stinging Fly.* His poems have been published in the USA in *Hayden's Ferry Review, Spoon River Poetry Review, The Hopkins Review, Psychology Tomorrow, Birmingham Poetry Review*, and *Éire-Ireland. Natural Bridge* nominated David's poem "Crash Centre" for a 2015 Pushcart Prize. (Managing Editor Mark Shaw wrote: "As an avid reader of Irish Literature, I found David McLoghlin's work … to be fresh and unexpected, yet still worthy of inclusion in the great canon of poetry that is produced by his nation." (Issue no. 31, Spring 2014) Most recently, he is the winner of Goodmorning Menagerie's 2014 Chapbook-in-Translation contest for *Sign Tongue* by Chilean poet Enrique Winter.

Majid Naficy, the Arthur Rimbaud of Persian poetry, fled Iran in 1983, a year and a half after the execution of his wife, Ezzat, in Tehran. Since 1984 Majid has been living in West Los Angeles. He has published two collections of poetry in English, *Muddy Shoes* (Beyond Baroque Books, 1999) and *Father and Son* (Red Hen Press, 2003) as well as his doctoral dissertation at UCLA *Modernism and Ideology in Persian Literature* (University Press of America, 1997). Majid has also published more than twenty books of poetry and essays in Persian.

Majid Naficy's poetry has been anthologized in many books including *Poetry in the Windows* edited by Suzanne Lummis, *Poets Against the War* edited by Sam Hamill, *Strange Times My Dear: The Pen Anthol-*

ogy of Contemporary Iranian Literature edited by Nahid Mozaffari and Ahmad Karimi-Hakkak, *Lounge Lit: An Anthology of Poetry and Fiction* by the Writers of Literati Cocktail and *Rhapsodomancy*, *Belonging: New Poetry by Iranians around the World* edited by Niloufar Talebi, *After Shocks: The Poetry of Recovery for Life* edited by Tom Lombardo, *Becoming Americans: Four Centuries of Immigrant Writing* edited by Ilan Stavans, *Revolutionary Poets Brigade Anthology* edited by Jack Hirschman and Mark Lipman, and *Al-Mutanabbi Street Starts Here* edited by Beau Beausoleil and Deema Shihabi. Majid is one of the six poets featured in the film *Poetry of Resilience* directed by the Oscar-nominated documentary filmmaker Katja Esson. He was the first writer in residence in Annenberg Community Beach House, Santa Monica in 2009–10, and the judge for Interboard Poetry Community contests in 2009. Majid has received awards in two poetry contests, "Poetry in the Windows" sponsored by the "Arroyo Arts Collective" as well as "Poetry and Recipe" organized by "Writers at Work" in Los Angeles. His poetry has been engraved by the City in public spaces in Venice Beach and Studio City. His life and work was featured in *LA Weekly*, February 9–15, 2001 written by Louise Steinman, entitled "Poet of Revolution: Majid Naficy's Tragic Journey Home." In January 2014, his Portrait was aired on VOA in Persian. Now it is available with English subtitles on Youtube: http://www.youtube.com/watch?v=okfGJgf4RRI

Marilène Phipps-Kettlewell is a painter, poet and short story writer who was born and grew up in Haiti. She has held fellowships at the Guggenheim Foundation, at Harvard University's Bunting Institute, W.E.B. Du Bois Institute, and the Center for the Study of World Religions.

Described by the *San Francisco Book Review* as "a force to be reckoned with in literary circles," **Shabnam Piryaei** is an award-winning writer and filmmaker. In addition to authoring the books *FORWARD* (MUSEUM Books, 2014) and *ode to fragile* (Plain View Press, 2010), she has been awarded the Poets & Writers Amy Award and the Transport of the Aim Poetry Prize, as well as grants from the Elizabeth George Foundation, the Northern Manhattan Arts Alliance and the Barbara Deming Memorial Fund. Her films have been screened at film festivals and art galleries in the U.S. and internationally.

Barbara Jane Reyes is the author of *Diwata*, winner of the Global Filipino Literary Award in Poetry. She is also the author of *Poeta en San Francisco*, and *Gravities of Center*, as well as the chapbooks *Easter Sunday, Cherry*, and *For the City that Nearly Broke Me*. She teaches in the Yuchengco Philippine Studies Program at University of San Francisco.

José Antonio Rodríguez's books include the poetry collections *The Shallow End of Sleep* (Tia Chucha Press/Northwestern University Press) and *Backlit Hour* (SFA Press/Texas A&M UP), a finalist for the 2014 Paterson Poetry Prize. His work has appeared in numerous journals and magazines, including *Poetry, The New Republic, Memorious, The Texas Observer, Green Mountains Review, Huizache*, and elsewhere. His prose has appeared in the anthology *Our Lost Border: Essays on Life Amid the Narco-Violence* (Arte Público Press), *Memoir(and)*, the Poetry Society of America online, and elsewhere. His awards include the Bob Bush Memorial Award from the Texas Institute of Letters, the 2014 Founders' Prize from *RHINO*, the 2009 Allen Ginsberg Poetry Award from *Paterson Literary Review*, four nominations for the Pushcart Prize, and the Clifford D. Clark Doctoral Fellowship from Binghamton University, where he received a Ph.D. in English and Creative Writing. He also holds degrees in Biology and Theatre Arts, and currently teaches writing and literature at The University of Texas-Pan American.

Matthew Shenoda is the author of the poetry collections *Somewhere Else* (winner of the American Book Award), *Seasons of Lotus, Seasons of Bone* and *Tahrir Suite*. He is currently Associate Professor in the Department of Creative Writing at Columbia College Chicago. For more information visit: www.matthewshenoda.com

Sun Yung Shin is the author of poetry collections *Rough, and Savage* and *Skirt Full of Black* (Asian American Literary Award), both from Coffee House Press. She is the co-editor of *Outsiders Within: Writing on Transracial Adoption* and the author of *Cooper's Lesson*, a bilingual Korean/English illustrated book. Her third book of poetry, *Unbearable Splendor*, is forthcoming and her edited anthology, *A Peculiar Price: New Writing on Racial Realities in Minnesota*, is forthcoming in 2016. She lives in Minneapolis.

Anis Shivani is a poet, fiction wrier, and critic in Houston, Texas. His books include *Anatolia and Other Stories* (debut book from Black Lawrence Press), *Against the Workshop*, *The Fifth Lash and Other Stories*, and *My Tranquil War and Other Poems*, and the forthcoming books *Karachi Raj: A Novel* and *Soraya: Sonnets*, both out in 2015. Books recently finished or in progress include the novels *A History of the Cat in Nine Chapters or Less* and *Abruzzi, 1936*, and a collection of essays called *Literature in the Age of Globalization*.

Ocean Vuong is the author of *Night Sky With Exit Wounds* (Copper Canyon Press, 2016). A 2014 Ruth Lilly fellow, he has received honors from Kundiman, Poets House, The Civitella Ranieri Foundation, The Elizabeth George Foundation, The Academy of American Poets, and a 2014 Pushcart Prize. His poems appear in *The New Yorker, Poetry, The Nation, Boston Review, Kenyon Review, TriQuarterly, Best New Poets*

2014, and *American Poetry Review*, which awarded him the 2012 Stanley Kunitz Prize for Younger Poets. He lives in Queens, NY.

Sholeh Wolpé was born in Iran, and spent most of her teen years in Trinidad and the UK before settling in the United States. A recipient of the 2014 PEN/Heim Translation Fund award, 2013 Midwest Book Award and 2010 Lois Roth Persian Translation prize, Wolpé is the author of three collections of poetry and two books of translations, and is the editor of three anthologies. Her most recent publications are: *Keeping Time with Blue Hyacinths,* and *Breaking the Jaws of Silence: Sixty American Poets Speak to the World.* Her poems, translations, essays and reviews have appeared in scores of literary journals, periodicals and anthologies worldwide, and her poems have been translated into several languages. She lives in Los Angeles. Website: www.sholehwolpe.com